An Eagle Rising

David Cecil Kersey

WestBow
PRESS
A DIVISION OF THOMAS NELSON

WestBow Press books may be ordered through booksellers or by contacting:

WestBow Press
A Division of Thomas Nelson
1663 Liberty Drive
Bloomington, IN 47403
www.westbowpress.com
1-(866) 928-1240

ISBN: 978-1-4497-8099-9 (sc)
ISBN: 978-1-4497-8101-9 (hc)
ISBN: 978-1-4497-8100-2 (e)

Library of Congress Control Number: 2012924226

Printed in the United States of America

WestBow Press rev. date: 01/04/2013

Dedications

To Mary, thank you for being the diamond in my ruff.
To Preacher Tomberlin, friends till the end.
Most of all, To Jesus Christ, thank you for the blood.

FOREWORD

The church will always have a bright and prosperous future no matter what the world and Satan try to do to it. However, what roles will our children play in the survival of the Gospel of Jesus Christ after our generation is past? As the end of time and the appearing of our Lord and Savior draws near Satan will stop at nothing to see our young people bound by his chains and deceived by his lies. We cannot let this happen. Our younger generation has the greatest potential of any generation before, and potential joined with prayer and sound biblical teaching is an unstoppable force that will bring salvation to the lost and devastate the plans of an enemy bent on our total destruction. Jesus Christ never has and never will be defeated and he gives that same power to those that serve him faithfully. If the enemy is to defeat you, he must first blind your eyes to the fact that if you have salvation through the blood of Jesus your victory is secured for eternity. Satan has no power over the work that Christ has done in your life. However, the power that Christ gives is of no value to those who do not except him as their personal savior and turn from their sins to serve God with all of their heart. We as the older generation and more importantly the church, need to evaluate ourselves to see if we are equipping our young people to fight the good fight of faith and hold on to truth come what may.

Being fought is a spiritual war and our souls and the souls of our young people are the spoils of war. If we do not train our children up in the way they should go, we are sending them to their own destruction. We must equip them with the word of God and show them that righteousness overcomes evil every time. The only way our children will ever have a chance of making it to heaven is if we as professing Christians start living what we profess and show them that they are not powerless over the works of sin. They can have victory over drug and alcohol addiction. They do not have to be sexually active in order to be cool and fit in. If the world's way is all they see; they will think it is the only way. The life we live in Jesus Christ will show them a different and better way. If we as adults take the time and show our children how important God is to us, then God will be just as important to them. Moreover, taking time to show them how important God is will show your children how important they are to you. If we do not make our children feel that they are important to us, Satan will be sure to make them feel important to him, if only for a short time. However, that is all Satan needs to ensnare our children for life, just a short time. That period of time you were offended at church and stopped going, Satan snuck in and told your children that if Mommy will stop going so easily, then going to church and serving God was not that important.

I have made many mistakes over the course of my life. This book describes a few of those mistakes and the price I paid for choosing the path I chose. This book also describes my road back to God and testimonies that no matter how far in sin you go, we have a God in heaven that is willing to redeem you out of that sin. Instead of staying out all night going to drunken parties, I now spend my time in study of scripture and reaching out to a lost and dying world. Reaching out to the younger generation is a passion that I cannot ignore any longer. I have seen needless pain especially amongst our teenagers and I refuse to stand by and just talk about what needs to happen. It is time to get up and do it. People think Africa and China are mission fields, however, no matter what country you enter, a prime field mission lays within a generation not the borders of a country. We have a great responsibility to raise this younger generation by the bible, not by government mandates. It is time we teach them the ways of God instead of the ways of the world. We need to turn off the TVs, open our Bibles, and tune into God. Many people boast of being leaders but there are few leaders left in the Christian realm today.

We as the church need to start praying that God will raise true leaders in the church that will lead people to God instead of to themselves. My name is David Cecil Kersey and I hope you will lift my name up to heaven when you pray and ask God to make me a true and strong Christian leader. A Christian leader will show people from God's holy word how to live a righteous and holy life before God. A godly leader will not walk away when things get tough. They will not give up on you when everyone else has. A Godly leader will humble himself before God and allow God to minister through him. Why do we need Godly leaders today? The leaders of today train the leaders of tomorrow, and we need to start preparing the younger generation to fill our shoes as leaders of the church. The only way we can accomplish this is by getting God in them. Every time I have watched a movie about war, I have noticed one thing. When the bombs were exploding, and bullets flying, and everything looked, hopeless for the solder they all had one thing in common when that moment came. They performed their training and nothing else. That is what got them through and kept them alive. They would not have known what to do if not for their training. If we do not train our young people by the word of God, they will not know what to do when the enemy strikes the church or their life.

The right thing to do should come natural to our children if we train them right. The question is how many of us are willing to take the time and effort to train them. We cannot afford to shift the responsibility on this one. If they are going to be trained right, then people who have sold out completely to Jesus Christ and are willing to give what it takes to see this generation succeed should train them. Are you that person? Every true born again Christian should raise their hand on that one. If we have a church tomorrow it is because we trained a church today. Let us rise to the challenge and show our young people how to live for God. We have shown them how to gossip and backbite, now let us show them how to get right with God and then serve him. They deserve every drop of effort we put into them. It will not be easy training them but it must be done. They are waiting on us.

CHAPTER ONE

SILENT NIGHT

Silence, I love silence. Though I am not sure, there is such a thing anymore. Silence today means a place with not as much noise as other places, sort of a turned down version of ordinary life. When my wife and I were first married, we lived on the outskirts of my hometown. You talk about silence. The house situated down a little dirt road and tightly surrounded by mile high Georgia pines and a handful of neighbors who by all accounts, loved the silence as much as I did. You could sit for hours at night listening to the crickets chirp, and the whippoorwills sing, but it was not silent. We called it silence because we did not hear the sounds that the city could afford. However, tonight I believe I have heard silence for the first time in my life. Moreover, I cannot only hear the silence; I can feel the silence. It is as a place I heard described on T.V. one time. Scientists say that over the years there have been earthquakes and other disasters that caused buildings to collapse. Inside these buildings would be people trapped by thousands of tons of twisted metal and concrete falling on them, yet some would come through with only minor injuries.

Scientist would explain that these people survived by being caught in a pocket of energy caused by the falling debris. They say this pocket of energy would act as a force field repelling anything that tried to enter that space protecting the person from certain harm. I am not sure if this is really true, or just a theory of someone trying to make a name for himself, but tonight I would like to think of it as truth. My wife and I have had the life we are trying to build come crashing down around us. Yet there is something protecting us from the full effect of this near disaster. We have discouragement pounding us relentlessly, but we cannot feel the effects as in times past. We have failure screaming at the top of his lungs, yet we hear a distant whisper. We know a spiritual battle has begun. The pressure is trying to squeeze the life out of our walk with God. However, all we feel is silence. A feeling that God has his hands cupped around us protecting with his mercy and grace. We need help, but only God will do. We have questions that only God can answer. We have needs that only God can meet.

I can see God's hand all around us, but I also see something else. The soft glow of a full moon shines through the car window revealing the face of the closest friend I have next to Jesus, my wife, Mary. We have seen many hard times over the years and she has always stood by my side. A person that will stand by you when things get tough is hard to find in today's world of disposable everything. How many TV or radio repair shops do you see around anymore, not many? Why, because society today has taught us it is easier to get something new, than to endure hardships with what we already have. That is not Mary. Even when the call came in eleven years ago that I had been in an accident and may not live through the night, it did nothing to diminish the commitment she made to me on our wedding day. She would lay down the phone that day, pick up her determination, and come to the burn center in Atlanta. She stood by my side through it all. She would help the nurses teach me how to walk and use my severely burned hand again. In addition, she has a gift for using the right words at the right time, and she spoke words of life and encouragement into me.

However, tonight neither of us has any words. I think neither one wants to break the silence. A part of me hopes that it is never broken. We can do so much with today's technology, so why cannot this be the moment where I spend the rest of my life. I am not trying to hide from life. Life is the greatest thing I have to live for. I am not trying to hide; I just want to step aside before life runs over me with a busload of disappointment. I feel that in this moment of uncertainty I am about to find out who I really am. Have I been following the will of God for my life, or have I drifted into the dangerous seas of self-will? Has God really spoken to me, or have I been telling myself this is the right thing to be doing? In order to be honest with God, we must learn to be honest with ourselves. The moment I am speaking of happen to us as we were driving from the church we pastor in Everett City, GA, to our home in Jesup, just over twenty miles away. We have made more trips to the church than I can remember, and this would our fifth trip within a week. I am starting to wonder if I should have made this last trip. I did not feel like it in my body. My heart and soul is to do the work of the lord and to minister to those who are lost, but for the past eleven years, the pain in my body has grown worse, especially in the past several months.

Moreover, this trip to the church I have dubbed the preacher maker or breaker, even though it is not just for preachers, but also for anyone who is a born again believer in Jesus Christ. It has revealed to us that foreclosure had began on the building we are leasing to have church in and is scheduled for auction in two weeks. You can imagine our shock and dismay at this news especially when this building is the only one in the community that is unoccupied, or in usable condition. Mary and I have always believed God sent us to this place, so how could things be going wrong? Is God telling me that I made a mistake and am now living outside of his will? We may all have times like this in our Christian walk. Times when we have to decide if we really mean what we say when we call our self a Christian. In time like these, we can find out if God is having his way in our life or not. I have been praying that I would keep myself out of the way and allow God full control to do what he wants through my life. Matthew 16:25 teaches us that "For whosoever will save his life shall loose it: and whosoever will loose his life for my sake shall find it." (KJV) This is what I want for my life. To loose my life to God, so he can give it to me the way he intends me to have it. I am tired of getting in the way of what God is trying to do. I have found that we can have the best intentions in the world, and still get out of the will of the Father. I do not want this happening in my life. I want it Gods way or no way. I have three children at home who are depending on me to let God have his way with my life. They will never experience what it is like to grow up in a Christian home until I surrender fully to the will of the Father. I have to get me out of the way. This is what has brought me to this moment. This is a decisive moment.

When we have times as this, God can use it to draw us closer to him. One of the ways that God draws us closer to him is by removing the things that are separating us. However, a problem occurs when He does this. God begins removing things that are separating us from him, but we stick things back in those places before God can finish his work. I have been through things and God was removing selfish pride out of my life. Before he could finish I would stick bitterness there. He would remove unforgiveness, for me to replace it with anger. I have been praying that whatever God wants to do; I will be a willing vessel for him. Ultimately, how my life turns out is my decision. The Bible says in James 4:7-8 "Submit yourselves therefore to God. Resist the devil and he will flee from you. Draw nigh to God, and he will draw nigh to you". (KJV) This portion of scripture has three actions we must decide whether to do or not. We must submit, resist, and draw nigh. All of which involve us making a decision, and then acting upon that decision. Submitting and resisting is pushing unwanted things from our life. Then we make our greatest decision and draw nigh unto God. The more unwanted things I release, the tighter the grip I have on God. Prayer helps me release those unwanted things, and draws me closer to God. Prayer keeps me honest about who I am and what type of life I am living. My prayers are the blue print of my life. Whatever is at my door now, is here to find out if I really want what I have been praying. Am I willing to pay the price that comes with the fulfillment of that prayer? We say a prayer and we want it answered. Nevertheless, what happens between the asking and receiving is what makes the people of God who they are today. Mary has taught me lot about prayer. We cannot just say a prayer and then go on vacation from that prayer. We have to stick it out and see that prayer through.

There is a life to be lived after the prayer. We cannot just pray for our children's salvation. We have to live a redeemed life in front of them to accompany that prayer. We cannot just pray for someone's poverty; we have to give to relieve that poverty. My wife prayed for my soul for many years. However, the life that accompanied her prayers made the difference. Moreover, we must have faith in God while we pray. James 1:6-7 says "But let him ask in faith, not wavering. For he that wavereth is like a wave of the sea driven with the wind and tossed. For let not that man think he shall receive any thing of the Lord". (KJV) We need to put some walking shoes on our faith in God, and keep it in action at all times. Faith is not something I muster up when tragedy strikes. It should always be active and flowing in our life. In addition, we must remember that prayer is what keeps faith flowing through us consistently. E. M. Bounds once wrote "To have prayed well is to have studied well, more than that, to have prayed well is to have fought well, to have prayed well is to have lived well, to pray well is to die well". Andrew Murray went on to say, "Prayer not only teaches and strengthens us to work; work teaches and strengthens us to pray". These men of God are telling us something. If we are going to invest time in prayer; then we need to have the faith to get up and put that prayer into action. Our faith in Jesus Christ is the greatest gift that we can offer humanity. Nothing we do in this life matters without a heart-rooted faith in Jesus Christ. Nothing will change the lives of lost people around us without our faith in Jesus Christ. Consider for a moment what the scripture teaches in 1 Peter 1:7 "That the trial of your faith, being much more precious than of gold and silver that perishes, though it be tried with fire, might be found unto the praise and honor and glory at the appearing of Jesus Christ." (KJV)

People think that silver and gold are the most precious things in the world. However, if you removed all of the saints of God off the planet, they would soon find out how precious our faith is to them. This world would be in total disaster without the faith and prayers of the saints. And this world is doing all it can to silence those prayers, and turn our faith to other things. Look at the condition of our country. I believe we live in the greatest country in the world, however, our country needs the faith and prayers of Christians more now than it ever has. We need God to lead our Leaders. They say a vote is the most important thing you will do for your country, however, we need to pray before and after the vote. Our prayers can outreach our lifetime to a generation that has not been born yet. We must be vigilant in prayer; and keep our faith in a state of the safety off, and finger on the trigger. That is why Mary and I are walking through a trial right now. We refuse to let the stench of mothballs saturate our faith. We pulled it out of storage long ago, and we plan to keep it active in the trials, and every aspect of our life. Faith is telling me that God is bigger than any problem I can face. In addition, once I get through the challenge in front of me, my faith will be that much stronger.

You may say, "I don't need that kind of faith in my life", but let me invite you to look at our world today. Where I live, groceries have sky rocketed, along with gas, electric bills, water bills, taxes, and the kitchen sink. Our children forced to learn things in our public schools that do not line up with biblical belief and everywhere we turn our country removes God out of something, or so they think. Satan is making every effort to impress against the Children of God. It is time that we run down to the nearest hardware store and by ourselves a backbone and start living in front of the world what we profess behind the church doors. It is going to take all the faith you can get to accomplish anything for God. A lounge chair approach to Christianity will not cut it. Mary and I know we need all the faith that you can get, especially now. This last trip to the church has been more than just getting from point A to point B; it has been a journey for our very existence. This straw has the camel going to the chiropractor three times a week. We have put so much prayer and effort into this building. This may not seem like a big deal to some people, but they have not traveled the journey we have. We did not just come to this building; we came to this community. We came here with nothing to our name except a God given vision. A vision to see the power of God fall on a community in such a way, that it will break the chains of alcohol and drug addiction that is binding our young people.

To heal people who once served God, but have grown tired of the power struggles that often go on in our churches. To touch a people who have been disillusioned about God, and the true purpose of His church. To reach a generation who need to know that God loves them. In addition, there are still people here on earth that represents that love. To show them the love of God, instead of the judgment that comes from man. We have people coming to our churches that have been physically and sexually abused. They have stolen from there own parents to buy drugs and have been disowned in the process. They have committed crimes; and will forever be judged by society for there past mistakes. They have suffered at the hands of judgment, but it should not be the judgment of the Church. The vision God has given me for this ministry is to love and minister to people regardless of their background. I have seen sinners walk into church, then the church people would get out of earshot, and start criticizing them for the sin they are living in. We should love people regardless of what they have done, or doing. The love of Jesus says that it does not matter what man says about you, it is time to start listening to the one who created you. That should be the message of the church. Listen to God's voice, not the world's voice. The world has spoken many things into my personal life. I have suffered greatly at the words of others. People who should have been encouraging me have been my greatest source of discouragement. They have never missed an opportunity to hold high my past mistakes, and tell me how I will never amount to anything.

Now that I serve God instead of sin, they tell me how fat I have gotten since I stopped smoking and drinking. However, these words have had a unique effect on my life. They have actually pushed me in the direction of God to seek his opinion and approval of my life. God is the only one qualified to tell me who I am. He is the only one who sees me for who I really am, and how I feel in my heart. People make to many assumptions and that leads to an incorrect assessment of a person. We need to love people and leave the judgment to God. However, in reality, Christians are some of the most judgmental people on the face of the earth. We need to repent of this. This kind of behavior when gone unchecked causes people to feel unwelcome in our churches. I have seen people get up from the alter after giving their life to Christ, and they did not make it back to their seat before someone criticized them about the way they were dressed, or how long their hair was. The church should be embracing not casting away. Well meaning people can be our greatest hinderers. These people love to quote John 3:16 "for God so loved the world that he gave his only begotten son, that whosoever believeth in him should not perish, but have everlasting life". (KJV) However, they seem to throw the brakes on their reading abilities when they get to Matthew 3:17 "For God sent not his son into the world to condemn the world; but that the world through him might be saved". (KJV)

It is not our job as the Church of the Living God to condemn those who come through our doors, but to lead them to the Savior of their souls. I have seen people quote 1 Peter 4:17 "For the time is come that judgment must begin at the house of God." (KJV) They use this in order to criticize the unsaved people who come to their church. These people have sniffed too much pew polish. It is ludicrous to think that the great commission includes us passing judgment on the unsaved. You are saved by the grace of God. You did not do it, Jesus did. We as Christians owe our all to the Grace of God. Ephesians 2:8-9 "For by grace are ye saved through faith; and that not of yourselves: it is the gift of God: Not of works, lest any man should boast." (KJV) Be careful about judging the drug addict seeking help at your church door, doors have a way of swinging both ways. Moreover, I am talking to myself as well. That is why I stay on my knees and in the word so much. I have to stay in touch with the true purpose of why God sent his Son to die on the cross. I have been judgmental in the past. We cannot be effective witnesses for Christ if we have anything less than compassion for those who are lost.

One day I was reading Matthew and I came across some scriptures in chapter eleven that woke me up to my own condition as a professing Christian. Matthew 11:2-3 reads, "Now when John had heard in the prison the works of Christ, he sent two of his disciples, and said unto him, art thou he that should come or do we look for another?" (KJV) I do not want to get into why John the Baptist would ask this question to Jesus. When I read these words, it was like a bolt of lighting hitting me. I thought of all the people that I could have been a witness to, instead I left them asking the question, "are you really a Christian, or should I look for another?" Friend there should be no question in the minds of those around you of whether you are a true born again child of God or not. Matthew 11:4 says it all, "Jesus answered and said unto them, go and shew John again those things which ye do hear and see". (KJV) What is the world hearing and seeing out of us? What they saw and heard out of Jesus was proof of who he was. What they see and hear out of us is proof of who we are. I did not come to Everett City to make a name for myself, but to proclaim the name of the risen son of God. The only way I can do that is by living the life of Christ in front of them. 1 Peter 2:21 says "For even hereunto were ye called: because Christ also suffered for us, leaving us an example, that we should follow his steps" (KJV).

Are we truly following in his steps? Since I came to Everett city and started building a ministry out here, I have asked myself that question. I can reach this community no other way except by following in the steps of Jesus. I can get through this foreclosure no other way than walking in the steps of Jesus. Will we loose this building? It is possible. Will I give up and throw in the towel with Brush Arbor Ministries? Absolutely Not. And the reason I can not give up is I know if I walk in the steps of Christ I will always be needed wherever I go, because Christ is alive and well inside of me. No place on Earth does a Christian go unneeded while delivering a message of love from God. If Satan can do anything in your life, he will keep you blinded to how important your Christian walk is. The life that Jesus lives through you maybe the only chance someone has of being free of drug or alcohol addiction. A young woman may be starving herself to death thinking that it will bring her beauty, and then she looks at you and finds true beauty in the light of Christ that shines in your life. Our Christian walk leaves a very distinctive impression on the world around us.

We must always be ready to minister and be an example to those around us. However, be vigilant to allow your Christian life to flow naturally from God himself. Do not get in the frame of mind that you have to be a good person because that is what people expect of you. I see many children who grow up in the church living this kind of life. Become that good person by a true walk with God. Allow the Father to form in you a person who is genuine and faithful. If you try to act as a Christian without being born again, your life will collapse under the pressure. Only God can form genuine Christian character in you, only God can give you salvation, and He gives it through the blood of Jesus Christ. We have to depend on Jesus for everything in our Christian walk. We cannot live a Holy life apart from Jesus Christ. Moreover, do not let anyone tell you that you cannot live a Holy life. I have heard preachers tell people it is impossible to live a Holy life. You need to read and memorize Luke 1:37 "For with God nothing shall be impossible". (KJV) Then you need to know what the scripture teaches us about being holy. Romans 12:1 says "I beseech you therefore, brethren, by the mercies of God, that ye present your bodies a living sacrifice, holy, acceptable unto God, which is your reasonable service". (KJV) 1 Peter 1:15-16 says, "But as he which hath called you is holy, so be ye holy in all manner of conversation; Because it is written, be ye holy; for I am holy". (KJV)

You cannot do this on your own; God has to perform it in you. There is one thing that is lacking in every arena of society today, people who are genuine. You cannot be a Christian without being genuine. Christians are genuine by nature. We have seen politicians throw the Christian title around, however it seldom makes it past Election Day. We need to start praying that God will form us into genuine Christians. Out here in Everett City, we have no choice than to be true People of God. I have no family name to hide behind and no reputation that will buy me time until firmly established here. Jesus Christ is the only family name I carry with me, and it carries all power in Heaven and Earth.

Let Christ do his work in you. Do not try to do his work for him. God wants your faithfulness not your input. Let Jesus mold and make you into his image. God is the only one who can shape your true destiny. I often remind myself of a story that comes from Numbers chapter sixteen. The chapter begins with a man named Korah convincing two hundred and fifty men to rise up against Moses and Aaron. And these were no ordinary men. Korah was a Levite, chosen by God to stand before the congregation of Israel and make sacrifices for them. The remaining men the scriptures calls "men of renown" and "famous in the congregation". Numbers 16:2 (KJV)

These men rose up against Moses and Aaron because they wanted to be the High Priest along with their other duties. Moses tried to point out that they could only have the position given them by God. Korah had his position because of divine appointment, and so did Moses and Aaron who was the High Priest. However, Korah wanted the position of High Priest at all cost. Therefore, he tried to perform the duty of a High Priest. The ground opened up and he fell down into the pit. The two hundred and fifty men soon follow by fire from heaven consuming them. Only those appointed by God himself can fill the shoes of the High Priest. Did you know that you have a High Priest? The Bible tells us in Hebrews 3:1 "Wherefore, holy brethren, partakers of the heavenly calling, consider the Apostle and High Priest of our profession, Christ Jesus. (KJV) Jesus Christ is our High Priest now, and we must allow him to perform his duty in our life. We cannot live a life good enough to get to heaven without the blood of Jesus washing our sin away. If you are trying to get to Heaven any other way, except through Jesus Christ, you will destroy your own life. Jesus Christ is the only hope that we have in this life, and the next.

Look at the day and age we are living in. Why is there so much stress and distraction at Christmas time? The world is trying so hard to keep quiet the name of Jesus Christ. I have noticed something about people today. I can go out into public and say God, and most people will feel comfortable enough to listen and even carry on a conversation. The word God has become a general term in our society. However, when I say the name of Jesus, people get uneasy. The world does not want to hear that name anymore. That name will change everything if a person will let it. John 20:31 says "But these are written, that ye might believe that Jesus is the Christ, the Son of God, and that believing ye might have life through his name." (KJV) If Satan wants to do anything, he will try to keep quiet the name of Christ in your life. He knows if you ever call on that name, your life will never be the same. Even if you are a born again Christian, you need to call on that name everyday. Fall on your knees and begin calling on that name with all your heart, your life is waiting to be changed.

E.M. BOUNDS "E.M. BOUNDS ON PRAYER " WHITAKER HOUSE 1997

ANDREW MURRAY "WITH CHRIST IN THE SCHOOL OF PRAYER" HINDRICKSON

CHRISTIAN CLASSICS 1999

CHAPTER TWO

IS THE ENEMY DYING, OR DEFYING?

What we are doing at Brush Arbor Ministries means everything to my family and me. However, we have faced criticism for coming here. Our greatest criticism has come from the community itself, even though most of the community has welcomed us warmly. Let me give you an example of what we have faced. One Sunday morning, my wife and I were praying as we always do before a service. No one had showed up yet when this woman comes through the front door and confronts me. She says that she was on her way to church, when God spoke to her about our ministry. This whole time I was feeling uneasy about this person. God gives Christians discernment for times such as this. When this woman opened her mouth, she unleashed the most hateful attack against my family and me. She says that I had made a mistake placing a ministry there, and I would be closing my doors soon. She added that I could accomplish nothing in that community. Before I could say anything back, she rushes out the door placing twenty dollars in the collection plate. If she did not believe in what we are doing, then why did she give to us? Our actions have to match our words. We cannot believe everyone that calls them self a Christian.

Jesus said that we would be able to tell them by the fruit that they bear. Matthew 7:18-20 says, "A good tree cannot bring forth evil fruit, neither can a corrupt tree bring forth good fruit. Every tree that bringeth not forth good fruit is hewn down, and cast into the fire. Wherefore by their fruits ye shall know them." (KJV) If what a person says does not line up with the truth, it is a lie. Because the truth is, we had service after that woman left. At the end of the service, people where coming forward expressing their desire to be saved. Need I say more? It does not matter what people say about your ministry. What is God saying about it? If the Holy Spirit does not bear witness that what you are doing is of God; find you an alter somewhere and seek God with all your heart. We cannot lay claim to any success we have in the ministry, the Holy Spirit should be doing it through us. However, success is what people are looking for in today's society, even in the church. Unfortunately, most people will not give support until you achieve their idea of success. Their idea of success is not my cup of tea. All too often dollar signs measure success over souls saved. People who supported me over the years have loosened their ties with me. The building I am in is not their idea of success. They never ask of the souls saved here. When I am in a brand new building running a congregation of five-hundred, they will be back. For now, they sit quietly, waiting to see what happens.

I feel like David in the seventeenth chapter of 1 Samuel. This chapter describes a young David ordered by his father to deliver food to his brothers who were solders in the Israelite army. When David arrived in the camp of his brothers, he did not hear anyone praying or giving thanks to God for the victory. Instead, he heard the voice of an enemy Giant defying the people of God. His brothers were hanging around the tents afraid to face their enemy. It is sad that when the young generation showed up on a field of battle, he heard the voice of an enemy that should have already been defeated. This personifies many churches today. We have many things that we need to get victory over. However, we keep struggling with it never realizing that it is defying our walk with God. People hear from our struggles more than they hear from God. Nevertheless, when David heard the voice of the Giant, he felt the people of God should not be afraid. The battle is won, and they should face the giant knowing this. They were the people of God. What other reason did they need to be victorious? What other reason do we need to know that our life in Christ is victorious? Jesus said in John 16:33 "These things I have spoken unto you that in me ye might have peace. In the world you shall have tribulation: but be of good cheer; I have overcome the world." (KJV)

There is no greater power on earth than our faith in Jesus Christ. Faith in God, not a stone, defeated the giant. In other words, the spiritual, not the material things we hold on to, will defeat the enemy. The spiritual things that we hunger and thirst after make the impossible, possible, here in the physical world. Many Christians talk about defeating the giants in their life. However, when things get tough they are content going back to the tents and letting an enemy taunt them day after day. Church, the world is watching and listening to us. If all they see is an indecisive faith in the God we profess, they will have trouble believing the Gospel we preach. The world is seeing us defeated by giants we create ourselves within the church along with the unrighteousness we keep yielding ourselves too. Look at the relationship David had with his brothers. David faced a Giant that no one wanted to face, on a battlefield that no one wanted to walk upon themselves. However, when David showed a strong faith in God, his greatest resistance came from his brothers. Could you imagine what they would have said if David came back without defeating the Giant? "I thought you had faith in God". Or, "I knew you were out of the will of God all along". Moreover, the always inspiring, "I thought you were a true man of God". If you have time to criticize someone's walk with God, then you need to work on your own.

We as Christians should support one another, even if it means praying for someone in a different church, or denomination. People say, "I am not praying for them, they are wrong in what they believe". If I am wrong, then I need your prayers more than anybody does. There is sadness to the story of David and Goliath. The sadness comes when we think of all the men of God around David who were capable of defeating the Giant themselves. However, they had let their faith in God grow cold. They were all seasoned men of God who had fought battles David could not imagine. Yet, they saw this particular giant, and lost the will to fight. What is that giant in your life that you will not stand up against anymore? What has you hanging around the tents? I do not know what David brothers went through in their battlefield experiences, but God help us when we let our past battles affect us so much, that we will not face the ones in front of us. We allow ourselves to become sedated so we cannot feel the scars anymore. We need to let Jesus heal these wounds and become the people God called us to be.

This generation should be teaching the young people to fight the good fight of faith. Instead, it has lost the confidence in the God that has brought them through so much already. We talk of the power of God, but do little to show it.

When I was sixteen years old, I left my parents home to move back to my hometown. I lived by myself in a thirty-four foot travel trailer, and I attended a little church on the outside of town. While I was at that church, an elderly couple took me under their wings and taught me a lot about living for God. When I went to their house, they would always feed me. However, when the meal was over, they would sit for hours teaching me out of the scripture. In addition, this dear brother would invite me to his prayer room for a time of prayer. An invitation into someone's private prayer room was a great honor. We would pray for hours until the Glory of God filled the house. It was there I learned the importance of prayer. Some people pray because they cannot feel God. I pray because I have felt God, and desire him constantly. These people gave that legacy to me. They knew if I could get into the presence of God, I would always seek for more of him. They did not just tell my about the presence of God, they showed me the presence of God. The older generation has a lot to teach. I hope the younger generation is listening

We can learn from the trials of the more seasoned men and women of God. Nevertheless, we should not replace the voice of God, with the voice of man. The people who have had the greatest impact on my life, pointed me in the direction of God. Similar to the relationship Samuel had with Eli in 1 Samuel chapter three. Before Samuel came along, Hannah had never given birth to a child. She prayed, and God gave her Samuel. Things born out of prayer have the most promising future. After weaning, Samuel would spend the rest of his life in the presence of God. Eli would teach Samuel about the Temple, and to minister unto the Lord. However, one day, Samuel; would hear something he had never heard before. He heard a voice calling to him in the dark hours of the night. Have you ever heard the voice of God calling to you? Samuel went to his mentor to hear from him but Eli he sent Samuel away. This happened a second time, and Eli sent Samuel away again. However, when it happened a third time, we see the unexpected happen. 1 Samuel 3:8 states that "Eli perceived that the Lord had called the child." (KJV) In 1 Samuel 3:9 Eli tells Samuel", Go, lie down: it shall be, if he call thee, that thou shalt say, Speak, Lord; for thy servant heareth. (KJV)

Notice it says, "Eli perceived it was God calling Samuel". Where are the perceiving men of God today? Who is teaching our younger generation to listen for the voice of God? Who is teaching them to recognize the voice of God when they do hear it? That is what a true man or women of God will do for you. They will challenge you to answer the call of God in your life. However, the younger generation has a responsibility to keep themselves in a place where God can speak to them. Samuel spent his life in the house of God. He lived a life that was receptive to God. Is your life receptive to God? You cannot live in sin, and then blame the church because your spiritual life is going nowhere. Many will dedicate only so much of their life to God, and then blame the Pastor for the empty places in-which they struggle. Younger generation, it is time to prepare your heart for the call of God. Let the Holy Spirit do his work in you. Wait on God and let him call you when his timing is right. However, do not let anyone tell you that you can live in sin and live for God at the same time. They are lying to you. If we believe the Bible, then we cannot ignore 1 John 3:7-8. "Little children, let no man deceive you: he that doeth righteousness is righteous, even as he is righteous. He that committeth sin is of the devil; for the devil sinneth from the beginning. For this purpose the son of God was manifested, that he may destroy the works of the devil." (KJV)

If you sin, Satan is doing a work in you. However, you have a promise from God, that Jesus Christ can destroy the works of Satan out of your life. Do not feel hopeless when dealing with strongholds in your life. If you have an addiction, Jesus Christ can destroy that hold on your life. If you feel hopeless because you want to live for God, yet you commit that same sin repeatedly; not matter how hard you try not too; then quit trying to do it yourself and let Jesus Christ defeat it for you. However, do not except continuing in sin as the answer to your problem. Sin is there to destroy your life, not give you life. This generation needs to hear that no matter what is going on around them, they can make a stand for Jesus Christ. I hope we can raise a generation that fully understands this. A generation who embraces what Jesus says in Mark 10:21. "Then Jesus beholding him loved him, and said unto him, One thing thou lackest, go thy way, sell whatsoever thou hast, and give to the poor, and thou shalt have treasure in heaven: and come take up the cross and follow me." (KJV) We need to realize the cross spoken of here is an instrument of death. Jesus intends for us to take up that cross, die to the desires of the flesh; and follow him. Satan is not afraid of, and God is not pleased with people who try to live for him without dying to the desires of the flesh.

I named this book "AN EAGLE RISING" for an important reason. Before I started writing this book, a pastor sent me a message that said, "An Eagle rises above the storm. Rise above Eagle Man." He knew what I was facing in my life. He knew I could easily compromise my standards, and no one would blame me if I did. He also knows that I am a man who rather die than compromise. Therefore, he gave me the only advice he could give me. Rise above. That is who we should be. The church does not have to compromise biblical standards, and neither do you. We should rise above compromise. People are falling away from the church at an alarming rate. Nevertheless, that does not mean we have to compromise to keep people coming. If you give people a piece of the world to get them to church, you will have to give them more of the world to keep them coming. We have to give them God. God is the only thing that can change their life. It is time to draw closer to God than we ever have. If one person will give their all for Christ, they could change the tides of events in this world. Three things will change this world; faith in Jesus Christ, callused knees, and a well-worn Bible. Faith in Christ will change any life, and the other two will sustain that life in Christ. Prayer must have a prominent place in your life. If prayer and Bible study fade from your life, your walk with God will soon follow. You must build your spiritual life on the redemptive power in the blood of Jesus Christ, and you do that through repentance, prayer, and study of the scripture.

I am writing this book in almost unbearable pain. I have prayed eleven years for God to heal my body. I am not sure why he has not healed me yet. People have shared their ideas of why he has not, all of which; I can do without thank you. However, in all this pain, I can tell you from experience; whatever God does not deliver you from instantly, he will carry you through until the end. I wake up every morning with the challenge of facing the day in this condition. However, when I am finished praying, there is no doubt that I can make it. Whatever you are facing, face it with the Word of God and prayer. Some days the thought of facing a day of hard work in this condition is more than I can bear, and will I get off alone and cry. God knows what I am going through, and he sees me through every moment of that day. I could not make it through my life if I where not able to pray. Have a dedicated prayer life, and never forget to read the Word of God. When I face discouragement and do not know which way to turn, I go to prayer with my Bible open in front of me. I never fail to get what I need from God. I may pray and not feel the prayer answered, and then I would open my Bible and see the answer instantly. Prayer helps me understand the word of God; and the word of God shows me the need for prayer. Moreover, both help me know God more. The more I know God, the more I am at peace with what is going on around me. The more I pray and reach out to God, the more I can reach out to those around me.

The more I know him, the more I can love those who will never love me back. I can give to those who never give in return, and embrace those who pull away. I can bless those who curse me, and turn a cheek to those who hurt me. To love unconditionally is one of the greatest freedoms in the world. To do so, is to know Christ personally. I did something the other night I have never done. I went out into the parking lot of the church, and I knelt down and prayed for an hour. Cars were passing by and slowing down, but no matter. I want this community to know they have someone praying for them. I want them to know how much we love them. The prayers prayed in this community are some of the most important events that will take place here. These prayers will lead to salvation, deliverance, and healing. Things may not look good for us at this building. However, I know God did not send us here to fail. Christians are not people who quit when things look tough. We can always go to scripture to find inspiration in our time of discouragement. It is full of people who faced impossible odds only to come through better then they started. Look at the life of Joseph. God gave him a vision of who he was to become, and from that moment, his life seemed to take a downward spiral into grief and despair.

Joseph would soon enter into slavery, and he did it with the knowledge that his brothers were the cause of him being there. Time would pass and Joseph, recognized as a good man to those he served, would have his reputation tarnished by the deceitfulness of his master's unfaithful wife. Always faithful to the God he served, Joseph found himself setting in a dungeon because of that same faithfulness. However, as time went by, he rose to the top amongst all the prisoners. Moreover, after years of mistreatment by nearly everyone he had been faithful to, he found himself where he could be the most effective when hard times hit the land in which he lived. He saved the lives of all those who had done him wrong. However, he also saved the lives of those whom he loved deeply. Faithfulness is one of the most important characteristics of a true born again Christian. We have to be faithful when no one else will be. We have to be faithful to God, whether the world is being faithful to us or not. We cannot sink to the level of the world. Satan is always on the attack against our faithfulness. Just look at church attendance today. People are more faithful to their jobs, or their gyms, or their children's ball games then they are church. This world would be in better shape if professing Christians would be as faithful to God as they are their television.

It is a sad commentary to our faith in God when we sit in front of a television watching smut while our brothers and sisters in the Lord gather to worship God. I am glad Jesus is more faithful to us than we are to him. If Jesus were not faithful, we would not have salvation through his blood. He set the greatest example for faithfulness. Look at the final hours of his life. Luke 22:44 says it all for me, "And being in agony he prayed the more earnestly: and his sweat was as it were great drops of blood falling down to the ground". (KJV) Christ was so faithful to us that he suffered great agony even before he reached Calvary. He prayed that the cup might pass from him. A cup that was so great to bear, it caused his flesh to start bleeding under the strain of the moment. And notice when the agony came, he served even more earnestly. In addition, during that moment of strain, he asked for the will of the Father and not his own will. How many of us could do that? We had better learn to push past the flesh into the spiritual aspect of the circumstance. In addition, look at Luke 22:45 "And when he rose up from prayer, and was come to the disciples, he found them sleeping for sorrow." (KJV) While Jesus was preparing to redeem all humanity from their sins, and face a horrifying death in the process, the disciples fell asleep. I think this would have been the moment of truth for me. I have struggled with this sort of thing for the past several months.

I work so hard, and dedicate so much of my life to minister to people for them to not show up for church. It came to the point where

I had to fall on my knees and seek God for guidance in how I felt about people not being faithful in coming to church. So much work goes into preparing a church service that it is heart breaking when few show up. However, one day I had a breakthrough. I realized that I was being selfish. I felt these people owed me something for the time I had invested in preparation. They do not owe me anything. I have to do it as unto the Lord, and if humanity is not faithful to God themselves, that is their problem and it will show in their life. I have to be faithful no matter what people do. I had gotten were I was doing it for the people, and not for God. I am still working on this, but these days I do not wait on people to show up, I wait on God to show up. Since I started doing this, more and more people show up. However, this is not the end of the story about the faithfulness of Christ. After a time of prayer and agony, one of his own disciples would soon betray Christ. Then the remaining disciples would flee and leave him to face his accusers alone. How many of us could stand if everyone we loved vanished from our life at the first sign of hardship?

I hope you continue to serve God if this happens, because it could very well happen. Look at what Jesus says in Matthew 10:34-35 "Think not that I am come to send peace on earth: I came not to send peace, but a sword. For I am come to set a man at variance against his father, and the daughter in law against her mother in law." (KJV) Look at the picture presented here by Christ. This sounds the opposite of the Christ we know and serve, however, the sword he is talking about is a division that happens when someone of a household surrenders his life completely to Christ, but the others of the house will not serve God. Christ is talking here of someone who is so committed to Christ, that he will leave mother and father, brother and sister, to serve him. Look at who is being separated in v.35 "Man against Father" "Daughter in law against Mother in law". (KJV) Here is a man who wants to serve God, but his father will not allow it, so there is a division. However, if you take a closer look, it is not just a man, but also a man and wife "Daughter in law against Mother in law". Can you imagine this, a man and wife making a stand together for Jesus Christ? I get excited just thinking about it. It is an unstoppable pair of human beings.

This couple will have to make a stand and live for Jesus Christ without the benefit of the parents in the picture giving them encouragement. This is where I hope they have a good church body to help supplement what the parents will not give. If not, they should live for God anyway. They should be each other's greatest supporter. They should constantly pray and speak encouragement into one another. If you live in a home where your parents are living for God, you need to fall on your knees and thank your God. It is a hard thing to serve God without the full support of your loved ones, however, in some ways it can actually draw you closer to God. You must serve God no matter if your family and friends do it or not. Serving God is not a fad that you follow; it is a change of heart, and a change of life. Matthew 10:36-38 says, "And a man's foes shall be of his own household. He that loveth father or mother more than me is not worthy of me: and he that loveth son or daughter more than me is not worthy of me. And he that taketh not his cross, and followeth after me, is not worthy of me." (KJV) If you are going to serve God, you must love him more than you love anybody else in your life. God comes second to no one.

CHAPTER THREE

YES OFFICER THAT WAS MY GOAT

It is very important for us to realize like David did, that once we take our place on the battlefield for the Lord that we should never loose heart and go back to the tents. Listen to me friend, several years ago I pastured a church that almost made me change my mind about being in the ministry. Everyday I would wake up and ask myself "ok what is going to happen today?" Around every corner was someone waiting to let me know how unwanted I was. The actions of a few, not the whole church, tore down any progress we made. I would visit them in the hospital and would not get out of the building before they were phoning the other church members calling me a devil. I could not understand allowing these people to go on as they did, and everywhere I turned for help no one would help me. I felt alone and betrayed by my leadership. If you have ever felt that way, or feel that way now, then let me offer you some advice. It does not matter what anyone says or does to you, you still have to live the kind of life that Christ would have you live. Moreover, that is exactly what I set in my heart to do. I could not give up on what God had called me to do. So what if the people around you are hypocrites. That does not justify you becoming one yourself. And not saying that everyone who goes to church is a hypocrite because that is not true. Churches are full of the finest human beings on Earth. However, the hypocrites seem to make the headlines so to speak.

It does not matter what man tells you about yourself, you need to listen to God. If man's words do not line up Gods word, you need to send them packing. Again, listen to God. He may use an anointed man of God to speak to you, but it should still be God doing the talking. Be confident in your walk with God. Put all your confidence in him. David did. David knew that God was the only one who knew how he truly felt. David probably felt he had no choice but to succeed because he sure do not want to go back to the tents and hear what his brothers have to say about him if he failed. Its sad David's brothers did not encourage or even lay hands on David and pray for him, or even better, go out and fight with him. However, this seldom happens amongst Christians today. I love my brother and sisters in the Lord, some have stood with me when no one else would. I do not know what I would do without these people in my life. Nevertheless, I have had a lot who would not go the distance with me. People I dearly loved who did not understand the path in which God was calling me. If you have friends like this in the church, please do not get discouraged when they will not go to battle with you. They have their walk, and you have yours. Love them anyway, but do not let anyone discourage you from doing Gods will for your life. Just make sure that when you open your Bible you become the words you read in there, and the voice you are hearing is God's voice and not your own. Let God mold and make you with his words. If the words did not come from God, do not trust or obey them.

In addition, do not let the world discourage you from serving God. Your walk with God comes first above everything and everyone else. What I am about to tell you may be hard to believe but it is the truth nonetheless. The story begins in the winter of 1998. Mary and I had been married just over a year. I had started out our marriage with nothing but big dreams and her by my side, but with that, I thought I could conquer the world. I was working twelve to fifteen hours a day trying to make ends meet, but we still had very little money. The only car we had was a 1983 Chrysler Fifth Avenue that was given to me a year before I was married. We lived several miles back in the woods and I had to leave Mary at home without transportation while I went to work. I knew I needed to get another ride; I just did not know how I was going to do it. However, Mary was at home praying. One day while visiting her parent's home in Brunswick, her prayers would see the light of day. Her Dad mentioned to me that someone they knew had a truck for sale. They wanted five hundred dollars for it but he thought they might take less. Therefore, we drove to the man's house to look at it.

It was by no means a good-looking truck, but as long as it ran good, the rest would take care of itself. In addition, it did run very well. To put the icing on the cake, the man took one hundred dollars for it. I was on cloud nine, and Mary was happy to have a car at home. The only major problem with the truck was it did not come with a key. Instead, you had to crank it with a flat head screwdriver. This was not a problem for me at first. Although people asked how I kept thieves from stealing it, seeing how a simple screwdriver would crank it. I would reply, "Who carries a screwdriver around with them"? However, one day the screwdriver would become a problem. I was leaving work and when I crank the truck, the screwdriver slipped slicing the palm of my hand. It was time to do something different, so on the way home I came up with a plan. Now keep in mind Mary had lived with me long enough to know that when I said I had come up with a plan, she put the fire department on speed dial, and hid under the bed. She did not know this would the shining moment amongst all the plans I came up with before. The world was in for a rare treat.

We were building our house at the time, so I dug through some of the building material and found 2 light switches and some 12-2 wire, a recipe of genius. I ran one piece of wire from the ignition to a switch, and the other from the starter to a switch. You could flip one switch to turn on the ignition and the other to crank the truck. This worked very well for about three years, however it would eventually cause the truck to catch fire, and almost burn up. The good news is, many years have passed since then, and few people remember that part of the story. Now if I could just get my wife out from under the bed. However, before it caught fire something very strange would happen to us concerning that truck. I came home from work one day to talk with Mary for a moment and then head back to town. When I drove up, she was standing in the front yard feeding the goats and chickens. I parked the truck, jumped out, and headed towards her. Now picture this for a moment. I parked that truck at the top of a hill, exited the truck without shutting the door or putting the emergency brake on, even though it was a stick shift. I walked down to the bottom of the hill where Mary was, about forty feet in front the truck. We stood there and talked a few minutes. I was about to kiss her goodbye, when that truck crank up and came bearing down the hill towards us.

I felt confused by all this. I stood there with that "hey dude where is my car?" look in my eyes. I looked to my right and there stood nothing where Mary used to be. She had enough since to run for her life. When I looked back at the truck, one of our goats that hung out in the yard popped his head up over the dashboard. Everything became clear. I had left the door of the truck open and this goat had climbed in the truck, flipped those two light switches, and made goat history from there. I jumped out of the way and as the truck passed me, I jumped in and brought it to a stop. Now I have never seen a pig fly, but I have seen a goat fly down a hill in a Mazda pickup truck. There is a point I am trying to make here. Few people believe me when I tell them what happened that day. Nevertheless, it is still the truth. It really happened. When you tell people that Jesus Christ has saved your soul and you are no longer the same person you once were, they may not believe you. That does not mean it is not the truth. When you tell them that you no longer do drugs, they may say things like "I give it a week and you'll be right back on them". Do not believe them. The blood of Jesus Christ has redeemed you, and no drug can stand up against that.

You may have been in a sinful sexual relationship before you came to Christ. However, that person has no hold on your life any longer. The bible tells you in John 8:36 "If the son therefore shall make you free, ye shall be free indeed". (KJV) It goes on to say in Galatians 5:1 "Stand fast in the liberty wherewith Christ has made us free, and be not entangled again with the yoke of bondage". (KJV) Notice the words "entangled again", Christ has set you free, therefore; you never have to go back to those things. Do not let anyone question your salvation through Christ Jesus. Do not let Satan question your walk with God. Satan did that very thing with Eve in the Garden of Eden. Satan said in genesis 3:5 "For God doth know that in the day ye eat thereof, then your eyes shall be opened, and ye shall be as gods, knowing good and evil." (KJV) Satan presented the question to Eve" Is there something other than what is contained in my walk with God"? Eve got her eyes on something that God had with held from her. Once she ate the fruit of the tree, she found out why. People ask me all the time "why doesn't God want me to do this?" and I tell them that if God with holds something from you, it is harmful to you, even though you may not see anything wrong with it.

You must believe that your life is complete once you are in Christ Jesus. You do not need anything else outside of Gods will. Over looking, what we have, to see what we do not have, is human nature. That is what happened to Adam and Eve. Except for one tree, God gave them the entire garden to eat from and enjoy, but that was not enough. They wanted what God had with held from them. They over looked an abundance that God was offering, for a small portion Satan had. We sell ourselves so cheap. Your life is worth more than Satan is offering you for it. That is the saddest thing about sin. Sold into slavery means taken against ones will and sold. When sin enslaves you, you are selling yourself. That is why Jesus paid such a great price for you. He knew you were worth it. That is what redemption is all about. He bought you with his own blood so he could set you free. Free from sin, worry, depression, anger and ultimately save you from destroying your own life with sin. Now you are free to serve God as he intended.

Come what may we have to stand for Jesus Christ. I tell my children that it does not matter if they are the only ones left on the planet living for Christ; they still need to live it. You may be the only one in your family living for God, but keep living it. You may ask yourself "Why bother, I am not making a difference?" let me assure you that you are. There are people who are watching your life that you could never imagine. People not acquainted with you are watching, and you are making a difference in their life. When thinking of how our life affects those around us I recall the story of Elisha in 2 Kings 13:21. "And it came to pass as they were burying a man, that, behold, they spied a band of men; and they cast the man into the sepulcher of Elisha: and when the man was let down, and touched the bones of Elisha, he revived, and stood up on his feet. (KJV) What a testimony of the supernatural power of God that operates in the lives of his people. Elisha was dead and buried, however when a person encountered what Elisha left behind, the man came to life again. That should be the testimony of all washed in the blood people of God. Our life should leave something behind that revives a generation who are dead in there sins. Our life should testify that Jesus Christ died and resurrected on the third day so I can live a life free from sin. What is your life saying?

Stand for God when no one else will. This is what David understood to be the principle of his life. He did not care if everyone else was cowering by the tents afraid to take a stand for God; he was determined to break the mold. Are you a mold breaker? Satan has cast a mold and many of God's people have poured themselves into it. We must look to the word of God and remember that it says in Ephesians 2:10 "For we are his workmanship, created in Christ Jesus onto good works". (KJV) Its time we take stock of ourselves. We should clearly see who has the greatest influence over our life. Is it God or Satan? We need to guard against Satan and our flesh injecting ideas where the promises of God should be. We need constant reminders of what God has said concerning his people. That is exactly what David did. He asked in 1 Samuel 17:26 "Who is this uncircumcised Philistine, that he should defy the armies of the living God?" (KJV) David was quick to point out that Goliath was uncircumcised. Circumcision represented the covenant that God had with Abraham, and with all the people of God. David was reminding himself that he, and not Goliath; had the promises of God. In other words, he knew that Goliath was already defeated.

Right now is when the people of God should stand up with the kind of determination that David had. God needs a people who will take his promises to heart. In addition, stand on them no matter how big the problem may be, or how hopeless the circumstance may look. He needs a people who remind themselves of his promises on consistent bases. In addition, remind Satan as well. We need to remind Satan that in Genesis 3:15 God said "I will put enmity between thee and the women, and between thy seed and her seed, it shall bruise thy head, and thy shalt bruise his heel". (KJV) What was God talking about here? He was talking about his son Jesus Christ who would defeat Satan. Notice the location of the bruises. When he speaks of Christ, the bruise is on his heel, when he speaks of Satan, the bruise is on his head. Do you get the picture here? Jesus has his foot on the head of Satan. That is a promise from the father. Romans 16:20 says "And the God of peace shall bruise Satan under your feet shortly". (KJV) Look at what God is saying. Through the power of the cross, we can do the same thing. Just like in Joshua 10:24 "And it came to pass, when they brought out those kings unto Joshua, that Joshua called for all the men of Israel, and said unto the captains of the men of war which went with him, Come near, put your feet upon the necks of these kings. And they came near, and put their feet upon the necks of them." (KJV) The enemy of the people of God is under the feet of the people of God. We see this in the story of Peter who wanted to walk on the water with Jesus. When Peter jumped over the side of the boat and landed on the water he should have sank down over his head. Nevertheless, Jesus took what was over Peters head, and placed it under his feet.

I love the fact that Jesus walked on the water in the first place. I preach a lot about how baptism represents death, burial, and resurrection. How when we go under the water the old man dies, and we come up resurrected into a new life. Going under the water represents the grave. Jesus walking on top of that water shows us how Christ knew he was going to over come the grave before he got there. We need this kind of mindset. We are over comers of things we have not faced yet. However, overcoming the things we have not faced yet dose little good if we do not overcome what we are facing now. People live for years with things they should give to God the moment it happened. I have faced a lot in my life. My mother told me on numerous occasions that I have faced more than most folks have faced. I do not know if that is true or not. I could have done without many things that happened in my life. Called into the ministry at the age of seven, I can take you to the church and the pew I was sitting on when I felt that call on my life. I started studying the scripture every day. I wanted to learn as much as I could about God and his word. I felt such a burden for those who were lost in there sins. I prayed every night for the starving children over in Africa. I could picture myself over there holding one of those precious children and telling them about Jesus as I gave them something to eat.

I preached my first sermon on the day of my calling. We had an old Chevy conversion van, I put my Bible on the console between the driver and passenger seat, and I let my parents have it. I told them about Jesus dying on the cross and they needed him to save their souls. That was the only message I knew how to preach. It is still the only message I know. Sometimes I wonder if I had of taken up a collection that day if they would have given me my allowance early. All I wanted was to please the Father. I have never lost that feeling. However, one day when I was eighteen years old I made a decision that I hope you never make. I decided that I had put up with enough of church and the way that people act, and I would never go to church again. I had experienced some of the worst behavior I had ever seen. I saw things go on in the church that I did not understand. How could brothers and sisters in the Lord run each other down as they were doing? Why do church people gossip so much? Why was there so much division amongst Gods people? It was as if you had to take sides to go to church. Therefore, I walked away from the ministry, away from the church, and more importantly, I walked away from God. There is no good reason for leaving church. Men had done these things, not God. It was like hitting the self-destruct button. I turned into a full-fledged alcoholic. I started drinking heavily and partying every night. When I got off work, I did not even go home to change clothes. I would just head to the next party, drink until I passed out, get up the next day, and do it all over again.

During this time, I earned a reputation as a fighter and was beaten by a group of boys out side of a store where I stopped to buy some chicken. While I was fighting one group off me, another couple of guys jumped me from the side and beat me in the head with a chunk of asphalt. I lay on the sidewalk in a puddle of my own blood. You can see the scar very well on the side of my head. I was in fistfights, knife fights, and thrown in jail, all so I could try to fit into a world where I did not belong. That happens when someone tries hide from God in a world of sin. They never fit in. God's fingerprints will always be on their life. I drank more liquor, smoked more cigarettes, and cussed more than all my friends. Nevertheless, it was all to cover up the fact that no matter how hard I tried, I always felt out of place while living in sin. I had felt the power of God and was hooked for life. Sure, I got drunk, but it did not feel like God. I got high, but it was not him. I spoke the language of the world but I longed for his voice to speak in my life again. I went to a bar one night and sat beside a man and all we could talk about was God. He said that he was in church at one time and walked away from it all. We talked about how good God had been to us. As we talked, the conversation went to the behavior of church people. If we had it to do over, we would have never left, but deepened our walk with God. We realized that most church people where good people, however, a handful of bad apples have given the rest a bad name. We should not have let the behavior of a few people in the church interfere with our walk with God. We both left the bar sober that night. This would be my first step in a journey back to God. I started realizing then that I should have kept my eyes on God and not on the behavior of man.

My spiritual walk is with God, not the people around me. Sure, they had a role to play in my spiritual development. Nevertheless, the Father does the work. If man does not want to live the kind of life that can be an example to me, then so be it. God is what man can never be. God is what man will not allow him self to become. God will be that father that was never around, or that mother who was to busy with the drug addiction to show you any love. God can be anything you need him to be, and what you need him to be, is God. In addition, I would soon find out just how good God is and how far his grace reaches. I was lying one summer night in my easy chair and I could not stand myself any longer. I was making a life for my family and me. However, a life without a committed heart to God is no life at all. Everything means nothing. I was making good money and paying all my bills. My wife and I were building a house on a piece of land I had bought from my uncle some years earlier. A friend and I had started a small roofing company and jobs were coming in slowly, but consistently. I was driving a truck during the week to finance our roofing venture, and I would help the crew work in the evenings and weekends. From the outside, everything was as good as turnip greens on corn bread, but on the inside, I had a hurt that needed the hand of God to intervene. Therefore, at that moment, lying in that easy chair, I prayed a prayer that would change everything for me.

I poured my heart and soul out to God. I told him I was tired of living this kind of life. However, I just did not know how to let go of it. Caught between knowing what I should do and knowing what happened in the past, I asked God to do what ever it takes to get me free from the hurts of the past. I wanted free from the sin that was plaguing my life. I had prayed this prayer before, and within just a short while, I was over it, and would continue my life in sin. However, this time it would not be that simple. It was as if God was saying, "Son come home for good, and quit playing games". I got up the next morning with a lingering feeling that I was about to get a wake up call. I tried to shrug if off. I knew I had one load to take that day, and when I got home, it would be a night of card playing and partying with my friends. I would never make it to the card game, or any other card game for that matter.

CHAPTER FOUR

CAPTAIN AMERICA

It was the perfect day to be driving a truck. The sky was blue, the sun was shining bright, and there was good music playing on the radio. What else could a man ask for? I loved driving a truck. I was a third generation truck 'driver. My mother even drove a truck. I finished first in my class at truck driving school and I was living out my dream of eighteen wheels and an endless supply of highway. I had truck-driving coursing through my veins. If they checked my blood, they would have found half hemoglobin and half diesel fuel from Ed's truck stop down on U.S. 1. I would wake up in the morning and I couldn't wait to crawl up in the cab of that truck, wait for the glow plugs to do there thing, then fire that engine up and hear it purr like Percy Sledge singing a love song. It was a beautiful thing. I arrived at work that Friday morning, checked in with the boss man, did my pre-trip inspection, and headed to a truck stop. I got to the truck stop and filled the tanks with fuel, check my lights and tires, and then I put that truck in the wind. Few people could say they love what they do when making a living; however, I truly loved my profession. I could not wait to get up in the morning and go to work. Driving a truck is a moment-to-moment challenge and I rarely had a boring day. I saw truck driving as a service to my community and to my country. Rarely will you buy anything not brought to you by an eighteen-wheeler. The clothes you wear, the food you eat, even the car you drive, will see the service of an eighteen-wheeler somewhere along the way.

Looking back on this day some months later I would see things happen that could only be God working all around me. I believe he orchestrated things for me in a way that I could never imagine. Some would argue that God does not work in this manner; however, look at the life of Joseph along with other great people of the bible. Joseph's brothers sold him out to a land that would eventually be the salvation of them all. Only God can pull people out of their character and mold them into their true Christian character. I cannot deny certain events that have taken place in my own life that could only be God leading me back to himself. Take for instance, I am riding down interstate 16 and making good time. I feel like turning off the air and riding with the window down, as I would often do. However, this day I would do something I had never done even in a regular car or truck. I decided to not only roll the driver side window down, but the passenger side window as well. I cannot tell you why I had the urge to do this. Moreover, it was not an easy task. I could not reach over and roll the window down especially driving an eighty thousand pound vehicle. In order for me to do this safely, I had to pull over. I found a place to pull over, loosing valuable time; and I rolled the passenger window down. I would soon learn how vital rolling that window down would be to my survival. When I got back on the road all was right with the world. The wind was blowing in my face, and I could hear the tires humming on the asphalt. It was not long, I was pulling into the town, and just on, the other side was the drop site.

Maneuvering through town was not a problem. I remembered my boss man telling me to be careful on the road I was about to get on to because it was a little two-lane road with some sharp curbs. However, he had given me good instructions and I felt confident everything would go well. He had told me that I would pass the place because everyone, including himself, had passed it the first time going there. He told me of a place where I could turn around. Sure enough I passed it, but no worries, I would turn around and go back just like I was told. Coming up on the place I would turn around at I turn my blinker on and slow to almost a stop as not to drive off the drive way I was about to pull into. Then everything went black. I saw my whole life flash in front of my eyes. I saw my wife at home alone with my two children. I saw the times I had staggered home drunk in the middle of the night my wife worried sick over me. I saw me walking away from a church and never looking back. I saw a man who wanted more than anything to be a good husband to his wife, father to his children, and a good servant to his God in Heaven. A man who always fell short of what he intended to be. Someone who had big dreams for himself and his family but instead found himself living up to the low expectations of those who put him down.

I saw my entire life before my eyes at one time. I must say; I did not like what I saw. It was as if I was standing on the outside of my life, looking to the inside. I saw a man who I could not believe was I. I had ruined my life, and I was too blind to see what I had done. My hands are actually shaking trying to write these next words. In the midst of this revelation of who I had become and what I had done to my life, I had a pain that was so excruciating that it actually woke me from the vision I was having. It was then that I realized flames had engulfed my body. Friend there is no other feeling in this world like the feeling of your flesh burning off you. I could not believe what was happening to me. I looked around and all I could see was flames. Can you imagine for a moment walking away from God, and years later waking up and seeing nothing but flames. It was like God giving me a sneak preview of how life is for those who rebel against him. Considering this a wake up call would be an understatement. Many people might have started screaming franticly at this moment, but all I remember doing was looking around, almost crying, and saying one word, Mama. Nevertheless, I knew I had to get out of the truck so I looked at the driver window and saw something pressed against it. I turned to the passenger window and before I gave it a second thought, I dove through it; and landed head first on the ground beside the truck. Remember me stopping on the side of the interstate to roll the passenger window down. Who knew that would be my exit route even though I had to dive through a wall of flames to get through it.

It was then I saw a man approaching trying to help me put the flames out on my body. It had melted the soul of my left boot to the bottom of my foot. Once we got the flames out, I was in my underclothes, and part of my shirt. Remember your mother telling you to wear clean under clothes in case you are in a wreck and have to go the hospital? Well there you go. The skin on my left leg was gone. My head was bleeding so bad it drenched my upper body and torso. I fell into the arms of a man who then drug me to the other side of the highway. It was there that I asked Jesus to forgive me for all of my sins. I repented there on the side of the highway, me on one side, and my eighteen-wheeler on the other side literally burning to the ground. I am sure there are plenty of people who can sympathize with the way I felt at this moment. However, no one could have prepared me for the loneliness I was about to feel. As I was lying there, waiting for the paramedics to show up; I took a good look at the truck I had escaped from. It was then I realized what God had just brought me through that day. I did not know until that moment what had actually happened. I had slowed down to almost a stop so I could make a left hand turn, and just as I made my turn, another eighteen wheeler came from behind and slammed right into the side of my truck. We slid just over 100 feet hitting a light pole and both trucks caught fire. I could not believe I was still alive. Then I thought about the family I almost left behind. Then I realized that I might not survive the injuries that I had sustained. My family may never see me alive again.

I had to live through this. I knew that Jesus Christ had forgiven me of my sins, but if I died, my wife would live the rest of her life never knowing that I was now the man she was praying for me to become. I wanted the chance to thank her for never giving up on me or putting me down. I wanted the opportunity to show her the man I always wanted to be for her. I wanted the opportunity to tell the lost sheep of the world that no matter how far you have fallen there is always hope for you. God is not some lazy old man who is to sorry and fat to bend over and pick you up. We serve a loving a gracious God who will go to the extent of offering his on son just to see you saved. What God had done for me could not die with me on the side of the road; it had to go on living and passionately told to a world who thinks there is no hope left. I wanted the chance to show my children that I could be a good father and a good husband to their mother. Now I could do it through the power brought to me by the shed blood of Jesus Christ himself. I could not go back and change anything; however, I could go forward with my life in Christ. We cannot make things right by going back; things become right by moving forward on the right path. That path was now under my feet ready for walking upon.

I wanted my wife with me, but at this point, she did not know anything was wrong. What was going to happen to me? The ambulance had showed up, but they where saying it was no use taking me to the hospital. They carried me to a place where a life flight could land and take me to the burn center in Atlanta. I could see the worry on everyone's face. It was as if they where thinking to themselves that, even if I lived through this, I would have no quality of life. I could find little comfort in the words of those around me. I cannot blame them. I was in bad shape. My guardian angels were on life support. Therefore, I started praying again. If you read the scriptures, you will find a special breed of people. You will find people who trusted God when faced with the impossible. People who realized that what they put there trust in was the most important decision they would ever make. I knew that if I was going to make it through this, I had to put all my trust in God. Therefore, I did. It was then that something happened that I carry with me even now. Everyone around was looking at me as if they were just waiting for me to die, that was until the Life Flight landed. This guy got off the helicopter and began to speak, and he made me feel like I was going to make it. Every time I think of him, I think of one name, Captain America. That is who he looked and acted like.

I think about this when I am ministering to people. If we are looking at them like they are not going to make it, what does that say about the Christ we are trying to show them? Isn't it time that we start ministering with compassion and confidence that Captain America did. He made me feel that if death were the only answer, he would change the question. As Christians, we have power through the blood of Jesus Christ to change the final out come of someone's life simply by sharing Jesus Christ with them. We need to let the drug addict know that it does not matter how far down they have gone, there is always hope. We need to let them know that by themselves they are powerless over their addiction. However, through Jesus Christ they have all the power in Heaven and Earth working so they can live a life free from all addiction. I am not sure what Captain America's beliefs were, but I can tell you this. He made me believe that if I were going to die, it would not be on his watch. I hope and pray that Brush Arbor Ministries can send that kind of message not only to Everett City Ga, but also to the entire world. It will be accomplished one way and one way only, by preaching the Gospel of Jesus Christ and nothing else. If we are inviting people to church just to have the kind of numbers worth bragging about, then we are defeating ourselves.

If Captain America had shown up, jumped out of his chopper and said "well folks this is my three hundred and ninety seventh flight" that would have done me no good. His focus would have been on himself and not the person whose life was uncertain. The effect of our ministry is all about focus. What is our focus? Is our focus adding to our role book, or adding to the Lambs' Book of Life? Are we building congregations, or the Kingdom of Heaven? Are the churches we are building a testament to the blessings of the Father, or the pride and vanity of the men who are making the decisions around the church? Where is our focus? Is it money or souls? Is it popularity or souls? There is no multitasking when it comes to ministering to souls, our focus must be Jesus Christ and what he wants to accomplish in the life of the person in front of us. Captain America taught me a valuable lesson; self-centered people are of no value to those around them. Moreover, no self-centered person can make a successful man or women of God. We must realize that everything Christ did, or will ever do, is for our benefit. He saw past himself, into the eyes of every lost soul; and that is what motivated him, the will of the Father. You know what I like the most about Captain America. I never got the chance to thank him, however; that did not slow him down from doing what he knew was right. Doing right, for the sake of being right, is what motivated this man.

He dropped me off at Grady Memorial Hospital in Atlanta and I would never see him again. However, my life is a testament to the dedication this man felt for saving lives. The greatest testimony we have of what Jesus Christ has done for us, is how our new life affects those around us. Are we imparting life to those around us? I heard a preacher ask one time are you imparting life, or are you imparting death? My greatest fear is imparting nothing at all. To do so is imparting death. Jesus himself said in Matthew 5:14 "Ye are the light of the world; a city that is set on a hill cannot be hid". (KJV) The Savior that we have living in side of us should shine naturally in our life, not on one day, and off the next. I needed a savior on the side of the road that would stick it out with me, and that is what I got. I had some very hard days ahead of me. That is why the church needs to start acting like God intended for us to act. When someone gets up from the alter, their battle is just beginning. They need to see Christ in us just as much after conversion, as they did before conversion. God bringing me out of that fiery crash was just part of the miracle, getting me through every day after would be the greatest part. Getting people converted and then doing nothing is one of the down falls of the church. We need to learn that just as conversion is the beginning of our walk with God; it is also just the beginning of the churches work in the life of that new believer.

Look at the example Christ left us. Jesus Christ suffered and died on the cross to redeem us from our sins. This was the most powerful and important event in the history of man. God gave the world his only Son, and gave him as a sacrifice because man had rebelled against God. However, with the work completed on the cross, Jesus did not stop there. Jesus would then leave the grave after three days proving that he was the true Son of God. Then after walking the earth and instructing his disciples, he went to the Father to intercede for us. However, before he went to the Father, he gave us a promise. In John 14:18 Jesus says, "I will not leave you comfortless: I will come to you". (KJV) He did not give us salvation and leave us to fend for ourselves, he sent the Holy Spirit to be with us also. John 14:16-17 says, "And I will pray the Father, and he will give you another Comforter, that he may abide with you for ever. Even the Spirit of Truth; whom the world cannot receive, because it seeth him not, neither knoweth him: but ye know him; for he dwelleth with you, and shall be in you. (KJV) Why did Jesus do this? Because he knew, our greatest challenges lie within the days after conversion. Jesus knew we could not make it on our own. We need as much of him as we can get.

When Captain America dropped me off at the hospital it would be just the beginning of what I needed God to see me through. When I opened my eyes for the first time in the I.C.U. part of the burn center, I felt that God had blessed me by putting me in that place. The staff was so incredible. However, despite how well trained the staff was, they were still a tool in the hands of a healing God. That is why prayer is so important in the life of the believer, because at no time should man take the place of God in a persons life. I am there to lead people to Jesus Christ not to an organization or myself. The people that walk in our church doors need Christians led by the supernatural power of the Spirit of God. My first night on the burn center the doctor came in and said that my leg had swollen to the point were they had to relieve the pressure. A nurse came in with a tray full of instruments fallowed by a couple other nurses who gathered around my bed. The doctor gently leaned over me, looked in my eyes, and said, "You are the only patient on this hall at the moment so you can scream as loud as you want". Nothing good can happen after an introduction like that. He went on to explain that he had to slice my leg open to relieve the pressure. In addition, because of my brain injury they could not load me down with pain medication. He then took a surgical knife and cut my leg open from the knee to the ankle on both sides.

They were doing all that they could do to save my leg and they did a wonderful job. They spoke words of comfort while the doctor was working to save my leg. However, who do you think brought me through that ordeal? God did. He used the willing hands of those around me, but we must remember what the scripture teaches in 1 Corinthians 3:7 "So then neither is he that planteth any thing, neither he that watereth; but God that giveth the increase". (KJV) We must be willing hands in the hands of a living God. We must be willing to plant the seed of the word of God into people's lives, and then water that seed. Then we must pray and allow God to give the increase. Gods increase is worth more than a thousand of my words. The doctor walked out of that room not knowing if I would be able to keep my leg; or even live through the night. My wife called up all that she could call to get them to pray. She knew that the hands of the doctors were working on me, but that would not be enough, I needed God's mighty hand at work in my life. God never fails. Even though I would have to learn to walk again, I would keep my leg. I would face pain like none I had ever faced, but God saw me through it. I had the comfort that God would not allow more than I could handle. What ever I faced from that day on would have to pass through God first and get his stamp of approval. It would send us into shock if we saw the things that God held back from happening to us.

The Bible says in Isaiah 59:19 "When the enemy shall come in like a flood, the spirit of the Lord shall lift up a standard against him". (KJV) In Lamentations 3:22 the Bible says, "It is of the Lords mercies that we are not consumed, because his compassions fail not". (KJV) We should sleep well at night knowing who our God is, and what he intends to do for us. Let me share for a moment what God wants to do for you. I see so many who are sitting on church pews who think that God wants to forgive them of there sins and nothing else. Jesus Christ redeemed your soul not only so you can spend eternity with him in Heaven, but you can also have a better life while hear on Earth. Jesus said in John 10;10 "I am come that they might have life, and that they might have it more abundantly". (KJV) Listen friend, we need to get this message across not only to those who have recently came to Christ, but to those who have been around a while as well. Think about something for a moment. God brought me out of that truck alive. Burnt and beaten up, but I did make it home to live with my family. However, several years later something would happen and, unbelievably; God would have to rescue me from the same exact burning truck, but this time it would be even more difficult.

CHAPTER FIVE

REMEMBER ME

I love to get out and visit family and friends. I try to do it on consistent bases. There is something special about loading the family up in the Jeep on a cool autumn day, and taking a ride through miles of winding back roads. We stop at some roadside stand for a hot dog and a cool drink. Watching the endless miles of power lines for red - tailed hawks and catching a glimpse of a cubby of quall run for cover under some brush. Laughing and talking about our dreams and things we want to accomplish, places we would like to go, people we would like to meet. Just soaking in life and then at the end of the road there sits the people we set out to visit. Then on the way back home, you can enjoy talking about the good time we had visiting and how well everyone is doing. We might even pull to the side of the road to watch the sunset over the pines and see the sky molding itself into the color of red Georgia clay after a hard summer's rain. Most people stop watching at the first sign of stars in the sky, but that is when a sunset is at its peek. It is as if the sun is trying to get one last word in here, before it rises in another land shining on tonight's tomorrow. Going to visit people is a journey into the unknown. Seeing things, you do not see just setting around the house and talking to people who love you. Your life is your outlook of what you see, feel, and hear. People love to see you, feel you, and hear from you. That is why I like to get out and visit.

In the summer of 2005, I loaded my children up in my truck to go on such a visit. I have an uncle who lives out side of Vidalia, who was very sick from the onset of Lupus. I was going to stop by his house for a short visit, and then drive to my parent's home in Norristown

Ga, so they could spend some time with the kids. We had reached my uncles home and we stopped in the road waiting on a passing car before we turned left in to his driveway. I heard a sound over the radio. I looked into the rear view mirror just in time to see a truck hauling a load of logs come smashing into the rear of us totaling my truck out and ripping the hood off the eighteen-wheeler. Thank God for car seats. Both of my children came through without injury. All of us would walk away that day without any physical injury. However, I would walk away from that truck, and crawl back into the burning truck God had brought me out of four years earlier. I would go home that day, and I would not leave again for several months. When I looked up and saw that log truck in the rear view mirror, I knew what I was about to go through, but this time my children were about to go through it with me; and it was more than I could stand. I went nearly a year not being able to eat or sleep well because of the memory of what could have happened to my children. I can suffer all the pain in the world but it would not hurt me as bad as watching one of my children go through pain as I had. It was more than a man's mind can handle.

One night I was lying in my chair and God began to speak to me. He showed my how he healed a woman with an issue of blood. She had been this way for twelve years. He showed me a blind man sitting on the side of the road listening to people telling him to hush up while he cried out "Jesus thy son of David, have mercy on me!" Mark 10:47 (KJV) Then God showed me beyond the issue of blood, and the blinded eyes; into the heart of what motivated these people to reach out as they did. It was not the disease or the lack of eye site, but the emotional effect of their condition that caused such an outcry in these people. Do you hear the outcry of the world today? Are you moving towards that outcry with love and compassion in your heart? That is what we need in the church today; people you are willing to reach out to the emotional needs of those around them. Even though God had delivered me alive from that burning truck, I was dying inside after returning there emotionally several years later. I lived inside that burning truck for almost a year. It was time for God to bring me out and bring me out he did. However, I look around me and I see people who have chosen places in the past and are now living there. I see people who have lost loved ones who crawl inside a bottle to hide from the memory of what they have lost. They keep themselves numb with abuse of prescription drugs afraid to face their own heartache.

The church needs to reach out to these people. People who have returned from Vietnam unable to cope with what happened to them while over there. I cannot understand our attitude towards our solders that return from war. Did they mater only when they had a gun in there hand fighting in Afghanistan or Iraq or any other country we have fought in? We have p.o.w,'s who are sitting in their own living rooms right now, and walking by us at wall-mart, and kneeling beside us in church. An enemy that exists in their minds, but is just as real as the one they faced on a foreign soil has captured them. Moreover, one of the greatest challenges they face is coming home to a country that dose not understand what they have been through. Why can't we fight for their emotional safety, as they fought for our physical safety? They gave us peace of mind; now let us give them peace in mind. They need to know that they mater as much now, as they did while serving in uniform. In addition, I hope that Brush Arbor Ministries can let these people who are hurting know that you have a savior that can deliver you from any battlefield, wither in body or mind. You have someone fighting for you as we speak. Cast all your cares upon him. Moreover, your battlefield may be an abusive relationship, or the loss of a loved one, or suffering hurt by someone in the church. Its time to heal and learn to walk off the battlefield once the battle is over. This is one reason that I refuse to give up and walk away from Everett City, I have seen to many hurting people here. People who have fought for our country and made it out bodily but are unable to leave mentally. People who made it out of the abuse, or drug and alcohol addiction but now they do not know how function in life without these things. Its time to show them how to live again by teaching them about the cross of Calvary and the victory won for them there.

When I see the people that are hurting on the inside, I cannot help but see the thief that hung on the cross beside Jesus, and the words that he spoke. He said something very powerful that stirs my heart every time I read it in my Bible. In Luke 23:42 the thief speaks to Jesus saying "Remember me when thou comest into thy kingdom." (KJV) I love the image the thief had of Jesus. He saw Jesus as someone different from all those below him as he hung there. Society had thrown him away. He was hanging there so no one would have to deal with him any more. Soon to be dead, buried, and forgotten by all. The world saw a man who had done many bad things in his life. They wanted him to pay for those mistakes. Nevertheless, when he reached out to Christ all he asked for was remembrance. He did not say remember all my mistakes and the things I did wrong. Remember the man that got lost along the way. The man who wanted to go to college and make something out of himself, but had to quit school in the tenth grade to support a family by working twelve hours a day. A man who grew up in a bad neighborhood and felt the only way out was to deal drugs, which led to spending most of his life in prison. A man who went off to war not knowing what he was going to experience and somewhere amongst the death and war lost the ability to look at the world the same. The thief wanted Christ to remember the man who existed before the abuse, war, drugs, prison, alcohol, and all the mistakes that a man falls into in his lifetime.

That is the awesome thing about our God. When we repent of our sins and ask his forgiveness, he cast those sins as far as the east is to the west to remember them no more. He did not repair our old life; he gave us a new one. We are now living a fresh new life in Christ. That is what the scripture says about the work of the cross in our life. Psalms 103:12 says, "As far as the east is from the west, so far hath he removed our transgressions from us." (KJV) 2 Corinthians 5:17 says, "Therefore if any man be in Christ, he is a new creature"; old' things are passed away; behold all things are become new." (KJV) Here is a prime example of justification by faith in Jesus Christ. Imagine for a minute what at exactly the thief was looking at when this was taking place. Jesus was not by the seashore feeding the five thousand, or on the mountain teaching the people about being the light of the world. According to what Isaiah teaches us in Isaiah 52:14 Jesus was in very bad shaped and had been severely beaten by the time the thief got a chance to speak with him, "As many were astoined at thee; his visage was so marred more than any man, and his form more than the sons of men." (KJV) What the thief was looking at was a man who was put into the hands of the world, and then the world made what they wanted out of him. They could not change his Godliness, so they changed what they could, the physical, and flesh part of Jesus. What they ended up with is something that was unrecognizable. Moreover, that is exactly what happens when man gets his way with something. This is why we must live in the will of the Father; we only destroy things when we get our own way. When the thief looked at Christ, he saw a man who the world finally got their way with. However, his heart saw a God that no man can change.

The thief saw that man can destroy the flesh, but they cannot destroy the promises of God that lay beneath the flesh of Christ. What faith it took on the part of the thief to see what he saw in Christ. The religious leaders of the time could not see him for who he was. The religious crowd saw someone who wanted to get them out of there comfort zone; and they would not put up with that. The thief saw a redeemer. And guess who was redeemed, the man who saw past the flesh into who Christ really was. Moreover, we must pay close attention to the words spoken around Christ while he is on the cross. I read in Luke 23:37 that there were roman solders at the foot of the cross saying to Jesus "If thou be the king of the Jews save thyself". (KJV) These words may not seem to matter much, but words have a greater impact than we could ever imagine. Look at the thief on the other side of Christ. He would repeat the words of the Roman Soldier in Luke 23:39 "And one of the malefactors which were hanged railed on him, saying, If thou be Christ, save thyself and us". (KJV) That was the defining moment in that thief's life. One took his view of Christ from the world, and repeated what the world said. The other would speak what he believed by faith in Christ. He did not get his opinion of Jesus from TV, or some late night comedian. He would not go to some great professor at Harvard or Yale and ask his opinion of Christ. He believed that the man in front of him would soon be in his kingdom; and the thief just wanted to be remembered by him.

What a testimony of plain simple faith, and what faith can do even in a seemingly hopeless situation. In addition, when that faith is active in our life God does so much more than we can imagine. The thief, just wanting to be remembered, and Jesus looks at him and says "Today shalt thou be with me in paradise." Luke 23:43 (KJV) The thief never imagines he would receive what he did from Christ. If we can believe in Christ, then God will give us more than we could ever imagine. I wish I could get people to understand this. When the world gives you something, they want to give you as little as possible, even if you have purchased it. However, when God gives you something, he wants to give you the most he can give you. Moreover, what I see most in this story is the fact that the thief had no time to go feed the poor, or tell someone else what Christ had done for him, or anything else we do to exercise our faith in Christ. The thief was saved by the grace of God and nothing else. All he had to do was to believe in that Grace and he would spend eternity with the Father through his son Jesus Christ. We must put "works with our faith" James 2:17, 18, (KJV) but we are "saved by Grace" Ephesians 2:8 "for by Grace are ye saved through faith: and that not of yourselves: it is the gift of God." (KJV) In addition, Ephesians 2:9 goes on to say "not of works, lest any man should boast." (KJV) Friend it does not mater what condition you come to Christ, he is ready to meet you in your circumstance and save your soul. You maybe suffering right now from the effects of war, or abuse, or addiction, and you feel that the world has forgotten you and has thrown you away. Rest assures that God has never forgotten you. You may have forgotten him, but he knows your pain and the help you need to get through it. You must invite him into your life and believe that once you invite him in he will come and help you.

Do you believe that friend? Do you believe that Jesus Christ died for your sins, rose from the grave on the third day, and is now in heaven "standing on the right hand of God"? Acts 7:55 (KJV) If you confess and repent of your sins," which means to turn from your sins" and you believe the words in the sentence you just read, and then you are saved. It is your faith in Jesus Christ that will sustain you in your walk with God from now on. You have something now that no man takes from you. You are now free to live your life without the burden of sin. You have a new life. Let me speak from the heart right here. I do a lot of reading in a day's time. I am up most days at 4;00 a.m. praying and studying scripture until 8:00 a.m. when I get ready and go to work. When I get home, I spend time with my family and when they go to bed, I hit the books again. Despite the fact that I study a lot, I am not what some may call an educated man. I have never been to college. What I know about the Bible I have learned on my knees praying and by reading the Bible itself along with the works of men such as A.W. Tozer, Charles Spurgen, Charles Finney, William Gurnall, Ray H. Hughes, Charles Stanley, Billy Graham, Andrew Murray, R.A. Torrey, Jack Hayford, D.L. Moody, and more.

In my time of study I have come across some, "none of which I have mentioned" who look down on the less educated as if we should not be proclaiming the gospel without a seminary degree. Do not get me wrong, I wish I had the education of people like R. C. Sproul and some of these other people. However, you do not have to be a theologian to become a Christian or to tell the world of the work that God has done in your life. And as far as your Christian education goes, do not be ignorant of the word of God. Open your Bible, pray, and start learning from there. Find you a man of God who is teaching the truth and let the Holy Spirit use that man to further your biblical learning. And listen, he doesn't have to be preaching to five thousand people to be preaching the truth. You can travel the back roads here in Georgia and find churches deep in the woods with preaches who are hammering the truth strait from Gods Holy Word. In addition, a lot of them never draw a dime from the church but it does not stop them from proclaiming the gospel and meeting the needs of those entrusted to them. I love to hear Charles Stanley on the radio; he is doing a great work for the lord. Nevertheless, you do not have to be a Charles Stanley to tell people about Jesus Christ. Nobody can tell another person what Christ has done for your life as you can. However, what you do need is what Bro. Stanley has; let me explain. I work in a fabrication shop as a welder, and I remember one day we had the radio up and Bro. Stanley was preaching away on our need for salvation. I stopped welding, lifted my hood, and listened to what he was saying.

As I stood listening, I thought to myself that I have grown up listening to this man preach. In addition, I noticed that his voice was not quiet as strong as it used to be. Then I looked around and noticed something else. Some guys had walked into the shop without me knowing and all of our attention was on the radio. When the broadcast went off, every one of us said the same thing, when Bro. Stanley was preaching you could feel the power of God coming from the radio, and it gets stronger every time he speaks. We need to study the scripture as much as we can, but nothing can take the place of the power of God in our life. Bro. Stanley has taught us that over the years with his own life. And so have many other men. You do not have to know the Bible to be saved, but you should know your bible if you are saved. The word of God is my refuge, and it should be yours. Now that God has set you free from your sins, the scripture can teach you how to continue to grow in your walk with God. It can teach us how to continue to be victorious and that we do not have to fall back into sin when things get tough in our life. It will teach us how to reach out to those who are coming home from war and need the churches attention. It will teach us how to be a witness to those who think that Christianity is full of self-righteous judgmental people.

It will teach us how to show the love of Christ once again. to let the world know that Christianity is not here to condemn them. Rather, to show them a risen savior who has come to set them free from sin. Look at John 3:17 again, "For God sent not his son into the world to condemn the world; but that the world through him might be saved." (KJV) Does that mean that we should allow anything to go on in our churches, absolutely not? We have a standard to live by and that standard is the Word of God. Moreover, the greatest standard God has set for the Church is to love. We do not have to accept their sin in order to love them, and we do not have to hate them in order to not accept there sin. I have seen people who would reject someone who were homosexual, but they themselves would view pornography. Did we bump our head walking into the church or what? I do not agree with either one of these. Both need the blood of Christ applied to their life. It is my job to share the Gospel with all mankind; not to hate them because they are living in sin. When is the church going to learn to love again and quit acting like judge and jury?

If Jesus Christ had acted as we do sometimes, there would be no Christianity. Christianity is about reaching out to a lost and dying world and that is what Christ did. In the story of Jesus at the well with the Samaritan women, who are you in that scenario, Jesus or the disciples? Do you have a true desire to reach those who are lost, or just a desire for the title of a Christian? If you have a walk with God, then what are you accomplishing with your walk? If the life of Christ is supposed to be flowing out of you, then are you introverted when it comes to your Christianity? As we look at how Jesus reaches out to the woman at the well, look at your own life and see if Christ is able to work effectively through you. We come up with so many excuses about why we cannot minister to people. However, at the end of the day, if you are a Christian, then Christ should be able to minister through you. Do not let anyone tell you that you cannot be an effective witness for the Kingdom of God. You have a unique testimony; therefore, you have a unique way of reaching the lost. I have been around the trucking industry my whole life, so I feel comfortable at a truck stop preaching the Gospel. Your mission field may be a golf course, a swimming pool, or the local P.T.A. meeting.

I was on my way to church one morning and stopped at a local store to get some gas. While pumping gas in my jeep, a man walks up and starts digging through the garbage can near me. Then he begins to speak and what he says ministers to my need at the moment. We had little work to do at my job and things were looking very dismal with my bills and the ministry. I left home that day carrying a lot of question about how we could make ends meet, when this man looks at me and says the most extraordinary thing. He said, "Sir, I am disabled and the only work I can find is digging through garbage looking for aluminum cans". Then he said, "I feel like giving up four or five times a day, but I remind myself that I must carry on". And his final words hit me like a boulder rolled down from a mountain top. He said, "Digging through the garbage may not look like a great job, but I know people who are not even able to do this, I am a blessed man". He allowed me to realize that I may have ruff patches in life, but patches sown together make a beautiful quilt. This man's mission field was a garbage can at a gas station, and his testimony was unique only to him. I shook his hand then I gave him all the money I had in my pocket. He looked at me, smiled, and said that now he had enough money to buy some breakfast. We ministered to the needs of each other. I learned that where the souls of my feet touch is my mission field, and I share my testimony when I reach out in love to those around me.

CHAPTER SIX

MACARONI, CHEESE, AND CORN DOGS

There are many beautiful things in this world. I have a lot of beauty in my life. God has really blessed me. If we held a beauty pageant that my wife could be in, it could not be a Miss America pageant. It would have to be a Miss Galaxy or better yet, Miss Universe. In addition, she would still blow the competition away. She is better looking than fried chicken with a side order of more fried chicken. And God has blessed me with a beautiful and healthy family. And the greatest reason that I have such a beautiful family is because you can tell that God has his hand on their lives. There is something about the lives of people who trust in the Lord for there salvation. I remember something that happened just a month or two back that made me appreciate the beauty that God brings into our lives. We had been very slack at work, so much so that my Son and I loaded up our push mowers and road around town looking for yards to mow. We did not have much success here in Jesup, so we had to drive forty miles south to the town of Brunswick and work there.

We found enough work to keep us busy, but it seemed that every after noon a thunderstorm would pull in. After buying gas to get down there, we would only clear about forty or fifty dollars a day. I started to get discouraged about how my life was going. Then one day I headed to Brunswick alone to mow some yards, and I drove by this little church with the front door standing open. I stopped in thinking that the Pastor of the church may be there and we could share some encouraging words between ourselves. I have done this before with pastors I did not even know, and made some life long friends in the process. However, this time would be different. I walked into the church and I saw a little man kneeling at an alter crying aloud the names of what must have been his Pastor, and others he went to church with. Then he started praying for his family and he ended by thanking God for the simple things he had in his life. In addition, what made this even more precious was the fact that the man mispronounced most of his words, and probably had less education than most folks had. While I sat, I could not help thinking I wish this man were praying for me.

You could tell that whatever God had done for this man, he had gratitude like few I had ever seen. It brought tears to my eyes, and brings them even now to think of that little man who is a giant for the kingdom of God; even though he goes, unnoticed by most of the population. It does not matter who you are, once applied the hand of God cannot hide in your life. It is like the city Jesus spoke about in Matthew 5:14 "Ye are the light of the world; a city that is set upon a hill cannot be hid". (KJV) I have never seen a life that did not change once God came into it. That is who our God is, a life changing God. Moreover, the change that God makes in the lives of human beings is seen clearly, as we look at the story of the women at the well with Jesus in John chapter four. The bible says that Jesus was sitting by the well of Jacob, weary from his journey when a Samaritan women approaches wanting to draw water from the well. John 4:6-7 "Now Jacobs well was there. Jesus therefore, being wearied with his journey, sat thus on the well, and it was about the sixth hour. There cometh a women of Samaria to draw water: Jesus saith unto her, give me to drink." (KJV) This woman had carried a water pot quiet a distance before running into Jesus. It is just like Jesus to minister to us in the mist of carrying the heavy load. We seldom realize how heavy our load is while we carry it, we just focus on carrying it.

However, with the load removed we fully understand the service of the one who removed it from us. We can understand our true condition better when our condition has been changed completely. I appreciate my wife's cooking even more when I am extremely hungry than when I have had a Whopper on the way home. Do not tell her I had a Whopper on the way home please, she is a Big Mac girl herself. Nevertheless, the water pot was not the only load the Samaritan woman carried. The weight of sin was more than any physical weight she could carry, and that is what Jesus would address. He started by pointing out what she needed in her life. John 4:10 "Jesus answered and said unto her, If thou knewest the gift of God, and who it is that saith to thee, Give me to drink; thou wouldest have asked of him, and he would have given thee living water." (KJV) Then he pointed out that she was living a life contrary to what she needed to live. John 4:16-18 "Jesus said unto her, Go, call thy husband, and come hither. The women answered and said, I have no husband. Jesus said unto her, Thou hast well said, I have no husband: For thou hast had five husbands; and he whom thou now hast is not thy husband: in that sadist thou truly." (KJV) Then he revealed himself to her. John 4:25:26 "The woman saith unto him, I know that Messias cometh, which is called Christ: when he is come, he will tell us all things. Jesus saith unto her, I that speak unto thee am he." (KJV)

Jesus is trying to speak to this generation as he did the Samaritan woman. He is trying to show us that the life style of the world is not working for us and He is doing all he can to reveal himself to us. We need to pray that God will open our eyes to our own condition so we can see how many things we have put in the place of God in our life. He showed the Samaritan woman that the men in her life would never answer the longing in her soul. She and her people had worshiped many Gods and she had a failed marriage for every one of them. Jesus showed her that the only way to have true fulfillment is not by breaking in a new ex-husband, but by surrendering her life completely to God. Looking outside of God for the answer to life's problem is a certain way to live in failure. You are not necessarily a failure yourself; you just have not given yourself the correct options. The Samaritan woman thought she was doing the only thing there was to do until Jesus showed her another option. Living the Christian life is showing the world the correct option when it comes to living a successful and joyful life. If Jesus had not come along the woman at the well would have spent the rest of her days living an unnecessary life. However, when Jesus came along he showed her that she had another choice besides the sin she was living in.

I want to point out that even though Christ was tired in his body, he still fulfilled the ministry that the Father had called him. Jesus did not let the flesh get in the way of an opportunity to share his love and compassion with someone who other wise never receives any. He isn't hiding away in a church office somewhere letting someone else do the witnessing for him, he is out there in the trenches putting himself in a place where the lost can be found. It always amazes me how Christ can be exactly where we need him to be when we need him to be there. Moreover, this woman desperately needed someone to reach out to her. Notice where the disciples where when God is trying to reach out to this women. They were off getting something to eat, or in other words; tending to the flesh when there where spiritual matters to be taken care of. And some will say, "well they had to eat". Eating is just a metaphor for the bigger problems in our life. How many churchgoers would be telling someone about Jesus Christ at this moment if not for struggling with the guilt of watching pornography earlier in the day, or cussing someone out at the grocery store for cutting in front of them? In addition, how many would be reaching out to the lost except they themselves are so depressed they need someone to reach them. God has given us everything we need to over come all these obstacles, yet they are still getting in the way of the message the church should be getting out.

It makes me literally sick to my stomach at all the things man has come up with to try and justify sin in their life. I heard a youth pastor tell a group of young people that they were going to sin everyday, so all they could do was just ask God to forgive them at the end of the day. Friend, God did not redeem us so we could be helpless to sin, he came to deliver us from our sins. We should stop telling this generation that they have to sin everyday and start telling them that they can be victorious over sin everyday. Man always falls back to that age-old excuse "well nobody is perfect". This is a dangerous frame of mind for a Christian. No, I am not perfect; I blew my chance at perfection the first time I committed a sin; but that does not mean that its o.k. for me to continue in my sins. If it were true then we would have to rip Romans chapter six completely out of the bible, and that just for starters. Look at Romans 6:2 "How shall we who are dead to sin, live any longer therein"? (KJV) There is no way that man can hold his life up to scripture and justify sin in his life.

In addition, I have been in discussions with people about this before and the first thing they throw in my face is the question "are you saying that we can live without sinning at all? My question is, why does it have to be all or nothing? If I commit a sin tomorrow, it somehow excuses me to live in sin every day from that day on. In addition, many people will quote Romans 3:23, which says "All have sinned and come short of the glory of God". (KJV) If you use that as an excuse to keep living in sin then you need to take the time out to read the whole chapter and quit taking that particular scripture out of context. However, even if you do not want to read the rest of the chapter lets look at Romans 3:23 itself. "All have sinned", (KJV) not all keep sinning or have "come short of the glory of God" (KJV) not keep coming short of the glory of God. The scripture teaches us to repent of our sins, which mean if I sin tomorrow, I need to turn from that sin and stop doing it. Repent means to turn away. I pastured a church one time that had a Sunday school teacher who would use profanity around the church even when he was teaching Sunday school.

I went to this person and spoke to them about their use of profanity and other colorful ways they would talk. Their explanation to me was that they could live in sin as much as they wanted because God was going to forgive them seven times seventy times a day. If you look at Matthew 18:21-22 you will see that is not what the scripture says. "Then came Peter to him, and said, Lord, how oft shall my brother sin against me, and I forgive him? Till seven times? Jesus saith unto him, I say not unto thee, until seven times: but until seventy times seven." (KJV) The scripture says if that person sins against me, I am the one to forgive them four hundred and ninety times a day, which is a shame that someone would need that much forgiveness from me. What kind of relationship would we have if they needed that much forgiveness? Moreover, the scripture is not saying its o.k. to sin. It is trying to drive home the point that we should be a forgiving people. And Luke refers to the same topic but he goes on to say in Luke 17:3 "Take heed to yourselves: If thy brother trespass against thee, rebuke him: and if he repent, forgive him." (KJV) In addition, because I forgive you, doses not mean that you will not have to answer to God for what you are doing; it means I will not have to answer to God for not forgiving you. Besides, what kind of testimony will you have if you need forgiveness from one person four hundred and ninety times a day? We would have to hire a secretary to handle all your forgiveness calls.

Church, lets wise up, instead of begging forgiveness from each other everyday; why don't we rise above and start living the life God intended us to live. There is a woman at the well waiting. We need to be ready when our paths meet. Moreover, the greatest testimony about the Samaritan women is that when she got to the well she did not find a bunch of guys munching on macaroni and cheese and corn dogs, she found Jesus Christ. That is what we need in our lives. When people come across us they will not find us indulging in the flesh, they will find Jesus living inside of us. In addition, look at how Jesus witnesses to this woman. He relates to her a life that is better than the one she has, one that has life flowing into it, not sitting stagnated by mistakes of the past. Then he reveals the center of why life is not flowing, the sin in her life. He reveals himself as the Messiah she has heard about all her life. He is there to save her despite what she had done wrong. This woman had been married five times and I have had church people fuss at me because I invited someone to church who had been married more than once.

We do not serve a God that is going to condemn someone to hell for making bad choices in there life which led them to be married more than once. If Christ did not give up on this part of society, then neither am I. Don't, get me wrong, I believe with all my heart that if you marry someone it is for life. Marriage is still a Godly covenant between a man and a woman, and many today are not taking that covenant seriously. In addition, I still believe what Jesus said about marriage in Mathew 19:8-9 still stands today. "He saith unto them, Moses because of the hardness of your hearts suffered you to put away your wives: but from the beginning it was not so. And I say unto you, whosoever shall put away his wife, except it be for fornication, and shall marry another, committeth adultery: and whoso marrieth her which is put away doth commit adultery." (KJV) The church has a responsibility to preach about marriage, but the congregation has the responsibility of living what is preached, and we all have the responsibility of rightly dividing the word of God. As far as condemning people who have been divorced, the word of God says in 2 Corinthians 5:17 "Therefore if any man be in Christ, he is a new creature: old things are passed away: behold, all things are become new." (KJV) Who am I to judge a man for what God has forgiven?

I have seen Christians beat there children over the head with this divorce and remarriage issue so much, that the children would rather live with someone than marry them, eliminating the possibility of divorce. Moreover, this is at the heartbeat of why I started Brush Arbor Ministries, I wanted to open the arms of the church to anyone who wanted a relationship with God, without the criticism of inviting someone to church who had been married more than once, or was not the same color I am. We cannot build the kingdom of God by picking and choosing who comes through our door. Church we need to lay aside "all" of our prejudices and start winning souls for the kingdom of God. Jesus did not take a resume from the women at the well before he witnessed to her, he saw a soul that needed redemption and that was it. Love does not see the mistakes people make, or how much money they have, or what color they are. It sees a life destroyed by sin that needs redemption through the blood of Jesus. The church has enough enemies to its integrity without adding ignorance to the list. We need to obey the scripture when it teaches to be "Wise as serpents but harmless as doves" Matthew 10:16. (KJV) We as the church have not always acted in the wisest of ways. However, there is hope; his name is Jesus Christ. I am depending on him to reach those that need help. Because listen, I talked about the beauty I have in my life, but the greatest beauty of all comes from the woman at the well who was lost in her sins one minute, and being a witness for Christ the next. It makes my heart rejoice when I think about Jesus having such an impact on this woman's life. People, who had seen her make so many mistakes, saw a dramatic change in her. It makes them not only stop a listen, but also search it out for themselves. What a testimony of the life changing power of Jesus Christ.

We should have that same testimony when the light of Christ shines in our life to those around us. Our walk with God should speak so loud that everyone around should stop and listen, and then search out what we have, finding Christ in the process. Our life should be a blue print to those around us showing them not in words, but in action, the life that can be lived in Jesus Christ. I have seen so many people allow Jesus to come into their heart and change their life forever, and I never grow tired of it. It is like watching God form a human being from corruption, making them into an image of holiness and love. There is nothing as beautiful and exciting as watching a newborn babe in Christ take their first steps as a born again Christian. I just wish we could see more of it, and I believe we will if we stay faithful to prayer and Gods word. We must remain faithful to serving God. Someone's life in eternity is depending on you and me reaching him or her with the gospel of Jesus Christ. Let us start reaching out today, as we never have before. Let us move forward with a new since of urgency. We do not know when Christ's return is, and we need to remain faithful and go into the hedges and highways and compel people to come to Christ. We need to be vigilant in praying for those that are going into the hedges and highways. The person they find may be your son or daughter.

CHAPTER SEVEN

YOUR CHURCH, YOUR FIGHT

I want you to picture for a moment Moses seeing the burning bush, and then remaining on the backside of the desert giving up on what God had called him to do. On the other hand, Peter denying Jesus, and then walking away from the Gospel for good, never excepting the forgiveness from God for what he had done. Or Christ himself, never dyeing on that precious cross for our sins. It makes me shiver when I think about what state my soul would be if Christ had not died for me. All of these men saw beyond themselves into something greater, the will of God, and the effect of their actions within the will of God. They saw that their obedience to the Father would influence the lives of those around them for generations to come. I cannot escape that thought when I consider just giving up here in Everett City going somewhere else and preach the Gospel. I have had plenty of offers from other churches, with big congregations and a good salary. However, what is all that if I am not where God wants me to be? In addition, where else could I go if I left this place even one second before God wants me to. This is not a carrier decision for me; this is my calling from God himself. It is not easy facing what we come against being in the ministry; it is very hard on the flesh sometimes. However, getting out of the will of God would be even worse.

It has never been about the money for me and God help my soul if it ever does. It has never been about being popular. That would mean that I care about what man thinks about what I am doing, and I don't care much about man's opinion. I have to put my trust in the Holy Spirit's guidance. We need to do this first in our life. We need to allow

God to sort through and eliminate any confusion that arises in my life. God is not the author of confusion, but a God that gives me power and love and a sound mind. I may please one man with what I am doing, but I will never please them all. I just worry about pleasing God. I am not talking about men or women of God who give me Godly advice. It would be unwise to go through life without someone there to give me Godly counsel. I am talking about folks who are speaking from the flesh and not the Holy Spirit. People who seldom pray, and read their Bible, but think they are experts on how the church should be run. When our church building came under for closer people started saying that, I should have never come here in the first place. I feel with all my heart and soul that God has sent me here for a reason. If I give up and walk away now, then someone in Everett City will miss what God wants to do through this ministry. What if we had listened to the people who said that this for closer was a sign that we should not have come here to Everett city, and what if I had listen to them instead of praying and fasting and depending on God to lead the way for Brush Arbor Ministries?

Because listen friend, we have prayed and asked God for his perfect will to be done and guess what? We are keeping our building. Moreover, here is the funny thing about all this. We were virtually unknown before this foreclosure started and now everyone in the area is talking about the church on the river road that almost lost there building but stuck it out despite what was said or done to them. Friend it came down to the wire with all this. My wife must have made thirty or forty phone calls, and the day before the scheduled foreclosure auction transpired, we learned that we could stay in it as long as we wanted and not pay a penny more. It had spread around that we would not be having service that Sunday because we had lost the building, so some of the folks that did not want us in the community were sitting at the church Sunday to talk and carry on, having no idea that we still had the building. I have mixed emotions when I think of the looks on their faces when we drove up to the church, unlocked the door, and went inside. On one hand it makes me smile that we over came the opposition, but on the other had it makes me cry to think that these people acted this way and call themselves Christians.

Do we not realize what we are doing when we act this way? Do we know the effect of this behavior on future generations? Do we see that if we have love and compassion that we will pass on a legacy of love and compassion? If we act ignorant then we pass on a legacy of ignorance. Where will it end? I look around and I see so many churches whose congregations are getting smaller and smaller. The only people who show up are the deacons or elders, or people who spent their life in that particular church. However, few new people ever come, and when they do, they do not stay long. In addition, we keep blaming the way the world is going on how many people we have at church, but in many cases; the way the church is going is why people do not show up. When people get in each other's faces to have shouting matches in the isle of the church they should not wonder why there congregation is fading away. My father-in-law has spent nearly forty years of his life in the ministry and he can tell you some stories. Family members of the church getting into fistfights within the church walls, or people who want control of the church so bad they will insult and run off anyone who threatens their hold on that church. In addition, Deacons who will get up and walk out of church if a preacher dare preaches past twelve noon.

What if God is not finished speaking to the church; do you want the preacher to stop preaching just to suit you? He is accountable to God for what happens behind that pulpit so do not put his ministry in jeopardy because you can sit in front of a TV for hours at the time, but you can't sit in church for one. If our leaders cannot act like leaders, then they should not be in a leadership position. It is time for many churches to clean house. Time is too short to let unqualified people in the place where only a true leader fits. 1 Timothy 5:22 states, "Lay hands suddenly on no man, neither be partaker of other men's sins: keep thyself pure." (KJV) The laying on of hands referred to here is the ordaining of leaders in the church. The scripture is teaching us not to be in a hurry to ordain someone unless he has proven himself an upright and Godly person. The church should spend much time in prayer and fasting before choosing any leader. Many people will shrug their shoulders at this comment and choose their leadership for no better reason than they are the oldest people in the church. However, we cannot over look the fact that if you do not choose leadership anointed by God for that position, you are a partaker of their sin. You need to protect your church at all cost, and you can do it through praying night and day.

The Church is a beautiful and holy thing. The Church is a place where men can come and find refuge from all that he sees around him in this dark and dismal world. Jesus Christ is the light that shines through the darkness leading men to God, and the light that shines; it shines through the Church. When I become part of the Body of Christ, I become the Church, and when man sees good in me, they are seeing Jesus in me. The Church is a good thing, and desperately needed in this world. The building the Church gathers in is not the Church, rather the Church gathers inside the building and that is why we call it the Church building. However, the world is seeing things go on inside the church building that is not part of the Church. Men walk into churches everyday who want a say-so in what goes on in the Church. The problem is they want to run the church and act at church, the way they run and act in their own homes. Nevertheless, they are living a life at home that is contrary to the word of God. We as the Church need to put a stop to these people. If someone does not live, a Godly life then why let him or her make decisions for Gods people?

If you love your church then fight for your church. Do not allow ungodliness to run ramped, do something about it. Fall on your knees and start praying and interceding for your church. Instead of falling away from God and the church, let what is happening deepen your own walk with God. If people cannot show you how to act like a Christian then let them show you how not to act. Then you can recognize the signs when they arise in your own life. Remember Elijah when he thought that he was the only prophet left but God showed him that there were still "seven thousand left that had not bowed a knee to Baal". 1 Kings 19:18 (KJV) God has a people. He has people in your church, and in your community, and all over the world, which have an unstoppable desire to serve him. You are not alone in this. Do not let a few bad apples ruin eternity for you. You be the one who rises above. We have a God who is more than worthy of our praise and dedication. Moreover, not all churches have the problems described here but if it ever arises in your church, do not give up, but trust in God that he will bring good out of the problems. God can make your church stronger for having come through it. You must be the one who has faith in God for the strength of your Church body. Do not say, "Well its so-in-so job to do the praying and believing around here". It is your church, and your responsibility to pray and intercede for that church. Christ did not walk away from you when things got tough, so do not walk away from him or his people when things get hard. You are better than that. God has chosen you for a specific task. He has chosen you because you are capable of rising above the adversary and letting the Holy Spirit do a mighty work in, and through you.

In addition, remember what the scripture teaches us in Isaiah 54:17 "No weapon formed against thee shall prosper". (KJV) Whatever you are facing in your life or in your church, it is your choice whether you overcome it or not. God has given you every tool possible to overcome these battles but you must be willing to take up the promises of God and use them. Trust not in your flesh to see you through. If you fail, it is because you have chosen something other than God. You need to get up and choose God this time. Choose God in every aspect of your life. There should be no place in your life that is void of God. Often times before a service I will get out and walk through the community and enjoy the fresh air, and enjoy talking to people who are out in their yards or passing by in their cars and stop to talk. I did this the other day and had a wonderful time even though the mosquitoes nearly turned me into a skeleton. There are times around Everett city when you swat the mosquitoes and there's times when you run for your life. This particular day was a swatting day so I walked on a stretch of road right in front of the church that leads down to a swampy area. I came upon a beautiful scene of a large body of water with cypress trees growing in the middle so I stood there and just looked at it.

But while I stood there I remembered that there had been quiet a few water moccasins killed in the area within the past few months so I started looking around to make sure I wasn't about to step on one. The man across the road from the church killed a three-foot rattlesnake just a few weeks earlier. It still had me on the look out for them. Another thing I noticed, I was only about three hundred yards from the church, but because I had walked closer to the water, the mosquitoes were worse than they had been. And as I looked out across the swamp I thought to myself that we could eliminate some problems if that swamp did not exist. In addition, as I walked back to the church the thought came to me "what about the swampy areas of our life? What about the areas that brings death to our spiritual lives? I saw a picture in my head of God coming in and cleaning up our lives but we are steady clinging to it like a child whose mother is getting toys together for a garage sale that the child does not want to get rid of. God is not a bulldozer service that comes in and clears the sin out of one part of our life pushing it to another area. If he did that, they would become swampy places. God came to cleanse us of from all unrighteousness, not leave us with areas of our life that breed things that destroy us.

Why are so many in the church addicted to pornography? Because they have the swampy areas in their lives that keep breading lust and that lust keeps crawling out and taking them over and causing them to do things that they regret just moments later. And that's not all these swamps are breading. What of greed, bitterness, envy, strife, Malice, depression, hate, selfishness, pride, and a laundry list of other things. Its time that we as the church learned how to be whole again and start walking upright before God like he intended us to walk and stop struggling with things that should be covered in the blood of Jesus. Its time that people who call themselves Christians to stop making excuses for there sins, and start walking free from them. In addition, I have heard some preachers make excuses for sin saying that a man can commit adultery and still be a Christian and go to Heaven. The scripture teaches in Galatians 5:19-21 "Now the works of the flesh are manifest which are these: adultery, fornication, uncleanness, lasciviousness, Idolatry, witchcraft, hatred, variance, emulations, wrath, strife, seditions, heresies, envying, murders, drunkenness, revellings, and such like: of which I tell you before, as I have also told you in time past that they which do such things shall not inherit the kingdom of God." (KJV)

If a man is under a denomination, is the doctrine of that denomination wrong when that man stands up and tells people that they can commit adultery and still go to Heaven while living in that sin? Not if that doctrine does not agree with that man's view. That is what is happening all too often in today's churches. Our denominations need to hold the men of the pulpit accountable to know the doctrine of that denomination. Men are preaching but they do not know how to preach their own doctrine. And they certainly can't preach the Bible. We cannot afford to have preachers who are learning the bible while standing behind the pulpit; they should know it before they get there. And not only know it, but living it also. Do not misunderstand me, I feel like Charles Spurgen in that I will always be a student of scripture. However, we should know what we believe and know how to preach it from the Holy Scripture. We should know the Bible before we step into a place of influence. It does not necessarily have to be a pulpit. However, most often it is. Its time that the Holy Spirit start speaking to our churches again and for man to lay the flesh aside and let God have his way. Time is short, and the cost for failure is great, "so let us lay aside every weight and sin that is hindering us, and run with patience the race that is set before us." Hebrew 12:1 (KJV)

CHAPTER EIGHT

BRUSH ARBOR MINISTRIES

Let me take a moment to describe Brush Arbor Ministries. First, let us start with the name Brush Arbor. Most folks have never heard of a brush arbor even though many of our older churches owe their existence to brush arbors. Here in Jesup alone there are over one hundred churches. That does not include the sometimes hard to find churches out in the country. The population of churches here in the south is great in number, but it has not always been that way. Many areas only had one or two churches to serve the whole community, and that is where brush arbors came in. I spent a lot of my life listening to the older generation. I have visited many elderly people over the years and have spent hours at the time listening to them talk about the good old days. One of the things that I heard them talk about was brush arbors. They would talk about the revivals they would have and the people saved in these meetings. They would talk about how they did not have an abundance of church buildings as we do today, so they would have church were they could. A preacher would come to town and set up a brush arbor, which was made of the materials they had available. They would use scrap lumber or small trees they would cut down on the property, or use palmetto bushes for the roof.

Whatever they had available to build with, that is what they used. People received salvation then they got a preacher to come in who was willing to pastor the flock, and a church would spring up from there. There is a church just over twenty miles from where I live, and all the older folks tell me it started as a brush arbor. Moreover, many churches started this way, from just a simple faith in God and whatever they had available to build with there. That is the vision that God has given me for Brush Arbor Ministries. It does not mater how small we start out; something greater should emerge from it. In addition, I believe that is what kept our forefathers preaching the Gospel of Jesus Christ. They saw something greater than what could be seen at the moment. They believed if they stayed faithful to God, the seed they were planting would blossom into a fruitful orchard, and generations could come and feast from it. Friend, we must believe as they did. The seed planted, and what watering is done along the way, God will always supply the increase. I remember when I was traveling around evangelizing, it did not matter if I was in my car or on my motorcycle, I always carried a small container of seed corn with me. Every church I went to, I would go into the churchyard, and I would plant a piece of corn there to remind myself of the work I was doing.

You may think it silly for me doing that, but there was something special about kneeling down on the ground in my suit, digging in the dirt with my own two hands, and planting that seed there. It is as if I had not dug in the dirt myself, I would have cheated myself out of a special experience that God himself had for me. As if God was saying that if I was going to be faithful to him, then I needed to be willing to go all the way and not try to shift the responsibility to someone else. We are determined to see the gospel spread across the world through this ministry. And that's who we are at Brush Arbor Ministries; people who refuse to let someone else do our jobs for us. Just think, there are churches all over Georgia with corn popping up around the church and they have no idea how it got there, but it's a reflection of the ministry now established in Everett city. At one time the building that we have church in used to be a store where people would stop and buy gas, bait, beer, and cigarettes before they went to the river. We are two miles from the Altamaha River here in Georgia, and many folks pass by this building getting to the boat ramps at the park. Many of the Brush Arbor folks testify of the fact, that they themselves have bought beer from the very same place that they now worship God in. That is what I am talking about when I say greater things should come out of what we start. God can make great accomplishments out of the most unsuspecting things. In addition, there are many unsuspecting things in this world. Just as Brush Arbor Ministries is an unsuspecting thing in the middle of Everett City Ga, you may be the unsuspecting thing in the middle of your community and family. Do not sell yourself short. To sell you short is to sell what Christ did at Cavalry short. He paid a great ransom for you on that hill.

There is one thing that you need to remember about the ransom that was paid. If the ransom that was paid for you were paid to Satan, that would mean that Satan was the victor because he got what he wanted in the form of some type of payment. God receives the ransom paid for you, not Satan. God was the one wronged by the sinful acts of humanity therefore God was pleased by the act of Christ dying on the cross, bringing humanity once again into fellowship with God. Who receives the ransom is very important if we are to understand how we should walk with God. God himself receives the ransom; therefore, we should remember one thing: Satan gets nothing. Moreover, we need to remember that as we continue our walk with God; Satan gets nothing. When we wake up in the morning and decide how we are going to live out our day, we need to remember, Satan gets nothing. When we kneel in prayer for that child who is throwing their life away with drugs, we need to pray with the determination that Satan gets nothing, including our children. We need to walk the streets of the community that we minister in, look into the eyes of those who live there, and declare to them that Satan gets nothing.

If Satan gets nothing, then stop giving him pieces of your life. Those pieces of your life that you have yielded to Satan, become strongholds in which he can spy out, and conquer the rest of your life. It is time that we put up no trespassing signs along the borders of our life in Christ and let them be written in the precious blood of Jesus himself: Satan is a trespasser in your life, he does not belong there. We do not make treaties with him and allow him even the smallest territory in our life. He is the enemy of our soul plain and simple. There is no waving the white flag at Satan in hopes of him sparing your life, he will take it from you, forget you, and move on to the next soul he can steal. Satan will do you like I have seen some men do to women, once they get what they want, they will destroy you, forget you, and move on to the next willing soul. We do not have to fall for these tricks any longer. We are God's people, and we are not up for sale. We are purchased with the precious blood of the Lamb of God, and God is not running a flea market. He does not buy and sell what he purchases; he keeps it for eternity. That is the message of Brush Arbor Ministries. You are not some hand me down that God throws into a pile then sorts out according to what you are worth. We are all worth saving, and if you will allow God to save your soul, he will.

We have a group of people at Brush Arbor who have had rough lives but refuse to give up. The church all over the world is a body of people who refuse to give up. Mark 13:13 teaches us "whoever endures until the end shall be saved". (KJV) That is what we need to pass down to the next generation, endurance. History has taught us some very valuable things and we should pay attention. Back when sails, instead of diesel or nuclear engines, powered our naval ships, many men would die on ships especially when the ships would travel into arctic waters. Studies conducted showed why the men upon these ships would die when faced with bitter temperatures, and little or no food. The results of the studies have made me revisit the alter many times to ask Gods guidance in discipling the younger generation. We do need to be making disciples. They found that all the men had faced the same hardships, but the young men were dying. It was not that they did not have the same equipment to work with, or the same clothing to wear, but they did not have the same will to survive that the older generation had. They had not faced hardships like the older generation, so therefore they were not equipped emotionally to survive. Their will to survive was not as great as the older generation. We need to start teaching this generation that no matter what they face, God can carry them trough it. I have noticed something about the mind set of my wife and I since we went through the foreclosure on the building. Things that use to bother us do not bother us anymore. We know that faith in Christ will see us to the other side of any trial. Can you imagine for a moment the anguish we went through when the bank foreclosed on our building?

It was bad enough that we were facing the prospect of losing our building after making the claim that God had sent us there. To add salt to the wound, many of our members quit coming after they found out. I can count on one hand how many people stood with us. It made my chest heavy every time I thought about how people had a banded us. However, the bible is full of men and women who had only God himself left with them when they stood there ground for what believed in. Look at the story of Eleazar the son of Dodo that we see in 2 Samuel 23:10 "He arose, and smote the philistines until his hand was weary, and his hand clave unto his sword: and the Lord wrought a great victory that day; and the people returned after him only to spoil." (KJV) This man stood his ground and fought the philistines even though all the other people of Israel had left him there alone. He fought until his hand was weary and clave unto his sword and it goes on to say that, the Lord brought a great victory on the battlefield that day. I am glad to know that even if I have to fight it alone, "as far as human beings are concerned", I can still trust that the army of God is standing with me. In addition, what happened after this man won the battle for the people of Israel is just what we see in the church today. The bible says that the people who had fled away, returned to the battlefield just long enough to take the spoils from the fallen enemy.

This man had fought so hard for these people that he did not even have the strength to enjoy the fruits of his labor before someone else came and took it. This reminds me of a young man who sat in the church and complained about preachers who push paying tithes and giving to the church so much. I agree that some churches beat their people over the head to much about giving money. I can name churches that I have rarely been in a service when they were not talking about the need for money. And the only reason they were in need of money is because they had spent so much on projects that was more about keeping up with the Jones than building the kingdom of God. However, the problem with what this young man was saying is that my wife and I had paid ninety percent of the bills, and I never saw him give one dime. That would not bother me except people like this complain the building is hot during service, but they want someone else to pay the light bill. If you are part of a church, and you want a nice building to go to, padded chairs to set in, and a comfortable temperature in the building, then you need to align your life with the word of God and support your church as a faithful giver. Do not let someone else fight your battle, and then you just reap the benefits. It may look good at first, but the true blessings go to those who are holding the sword at the end of the battle.

My wife and I have led the way in giving at Brush Arbor Ministries for one simple reason, I am not going to ask someone to live a certain way unless I am doing it myself. I remember when we first came here; the side of the building that is facing the road still had the advertisement painted on it from when it was a store. In addition, the two most prominent words were beer and cigarettes, so I needed to paint over it as soon as possible. The whole building was in need of a paint job also. However, month after month we would pay the rent and have very little if anything left over to buy paint. So one day my wife and I were sitting around the house talking and she looked at me and said,' I am tired of the material things that we have around this house, they just seem to be cluttering our life". That night I tried to sleep but I could not because of the words she had spoken to me. I prayed and asked God if we had become to materialistic. I did not like his answer one bit. God asked me if there was any material thing in my life that I was not willing to sell to buy paint for the building. I could not think of one thing until I walked out into my garage and saw my motorcycle sitting there.

Friend, I am a die-hard motorcyclist. It does not mater, hot or cold, rain or shine, I want to do it on the back of a motorcycle. I went everywhere on that thing. I would dress up as Santa clause on Christmas morning and drive a couple hundred miles on my bike delivering gifts to children in surrounding counties. However, as I stood there looking at that bike I knew that it had to go. I could not lay my head down in peace at night knowing that there was some material thing in my life that I was not willing to give up for the work that God had called me into. Therefore, I sold it, we painted the inside, and part of the outside of the church, and another church bought the rest of the paint for the outside. That is what this generation needs to see us doing, giving up everything that needs giving up, to see the gospel spread throughout the world. And I know preachers who would criticize me to the bone for saying that we should give up the material for the spiritual, but that's only because they have become materialistic themselves. Do not get me wrong, I would like to have another bike and I know God will supply one for me one day. However, this time it will be different, because I realized something after I sold my bike; God blesses me with material things when material things do not matter to me anymore.

When we "Seek first the kingdom of God, and his righteousness, then all these things shall be added unto us." Matthew 6:33 (KJV) Moreover, the spiritual things in my life are what mean everything to me. That is the first step in teaching a generation about endurance. The only enduring things in this world are the things of God. If you focused on God so he can give you a Cadillac, or make you a millionaire, your walk will always be a shallow walk. Those things are only feeding the lust of the flesh. The bible teaches us to with draw ourselves from those who think that Godliness is gain. "Perverse disputings of men of corrupt minds, and destitute of the truth, supposing that gain is Godliness: from such withdraw thyself. But godliness with contentment is a great gain. For we brought nothing into this world and it is certain that we can carry nothing out. And having food and raiment, let us be therewith content. But they that will be rich fall into temptation and a snare, and into many foolish, and hurtful lust, which drown men into destruction and perdition. For the love of money is the root of all evil: which while some have coveted after, they have erred from the faith, and pierced themselves through with many sorrows. But thou, o man of God, flee these things: and follow after righteousness, godliness, faith, love, patience, and meekness. 1 Timothy 6:5-11 (KJV)

In addition, look what it says after you lay aside worldly things and seek after spiritual things. "Fight the good fight of faith, lay hold on eternal life, whereunto thou art also called, and hast professed a good profession before many witnesses." 1 Timothy 6:12. (KJV) If you want to have endurance in your walk with God, then do not build it upon material things. This is a fight of faith, but not faith in material things. And here again, you may have to stand alone if you allow God to work in your life through these scriptures. I know too many preachers who are stuck in this prosperity mode. We must rid ourselves of this materialistic view of the Gospel. I believe that God wants to prosper our lives, but our eyes should be on the giver, not on the gifts. There is a message of prosperity, but too many have abused it for there own gain. I do not believe I should be wearing a three thousand dollar suit when someone in my congregation is living on a fixed income and hardly putting food on the table. Why am I eating at Red Lobster when the people I am preaching to are eating bologna sandwiches? If you are going to endure, and teach others to endure, we need to get past the material and focus on the spiritual.

Since I let go of the material things for the spiritual things, we have not had the financial struggles that we had at the beginning. We have seen God come through time after time. Materialism has ruined a lot of the witness of the church, but not all of it. However, if we are going to teach the next generation how to be a witness and endure the hardships that come with the spread of the Gospel, then we need to teach them how to pray and intercede for one another. We need to show them how to find the answer to life's problem in the word of God, not from the TV, or drugs and alcohol. I read an article that said that America accounts for most of the worlds prescription drug use. It is spreading to the church at an alarming rate. We wonder why our children, instead of overcoming obstacles in there life, are turning to drugs. It is because mom and dad are at home popping prescription drugs for every little problem they have. They have learned from our example. Please, if you have high blood pressure, take your medicine. However, let us not take a pill trying to bring joy back into our lives. It will help with the chemical part of the problem, but we need to let God help us face up to the root of our problems. Something is stealing our joy.

We never learn to endure problems when we medicate ourselves to the point that we stay in a coma half the time. I have so many friends who like me, got hurt on the job and put on pain medication. When I came out of the hospital after suffering severe burns, I could not stand the pain while on pain medication, much less without it. However, I noticed that the time I spent with my family, and the way I treated them had changed dramatically. The more medicine I took to get out of pain, the more I needed to stay out of pain. In addition, I noticed the same things with my friends who are in the shape I was. People, who were healthy strong men, are now frail and skinny, unable to function throughout the day without a handful of pills. It is becoming a serious problem. We need to reach out to those who are facing this problem. I came off the pain medication, and now use diet and exercise to help with the pain. It is a great challenge to face a life of pain without the use of narcotics, but the benefits are overwhelming. My quality of life has improved despite facing chronic pain everyday. If I need something, I use over the counter pain relievers and even then, I am very carful to read and follow the label. Medication may do many good things, but it has done a lot of harm in the hands of those who use it to long, or in the wrong manner. Too many are abusing what the doctor intends for good. We cannot use medication in the place of strong moral values and coping skills when teaching the next generation how to live and be productive members of society, the church, and the Kingdom of God. We need to teach them how face up to their problems, not mask them with synthetic emotions. We have a generation so medicated that when they cannot get the medication from the doctor anymore, they turn to street drugs. I see it all the time.

We, as society, are turning our kids into drug addicts by abusing a drug that should be helping us. Let us fill this generations mind and soul with the over coming power of the Holy Spirit. Let us show them that no man made product can help them as God can. Let us show them that one of the greatest gifts that God has given us is our mind and the capacity to think. Drugs are destroying that gift, and the mind is something that is hard to regain once it is lost. I know this next generation is going to do well, but lets you and I remember one thing. What we teach our children, is what they become.

CHAPTER NINE

MAKE A LEFT TURN IN ALBUQUERQUE

Friend, we as the Body of Christ need to pay close attention to the words of the younger generation. I am not sure if you have noticed, but they are trying to tell us something. The message is abundantly clear, practice what you preach. I have seen young people come to church discouraged because during the week they saw a grown up they knew from church, displaying a life contrary to what they profess while at church. These young people are not stupid by any means. They know if you are genuine in your walk with God. If they keep seeing fake Christianity, they will search elsewhere for fulfillment in their life. I have had to clean up the mess of to many who call themselves Christian. One of the hardest parts of being a pastor has been trying to explain the sinful actions of supposing Christian people, to a younger generation. I have learned from my own mistakes on this point. I know how desperately Christian people need live the standards they profess. In the early years of my ministry, I have displayed less than Christian character. I saw the affects of my actions on those around me, and I must say it bothered me deeply.

Every time I think about the example I am setting for my children and others around me, I remind myself of an extraordinary event that took place with my brother and me when we were in our late teens. I had moved away from home and did not get to see my brother that often. He was working long hours, and engaged to be married, so even when I went home to visit, I rarely saw him. So you can imagine my surprise when one day, I received a phone call from him. Unfortunately, he was calling to tell me of the sudden death of a friend with whom we had grown up. It came as such a shock to me. This young man was the same age as us, and we take for granted that the young are not supposed to die. Deeply saddened by the news, I took off work and drove the hundred miles south to my brother's house. At the funeral the next day, so many people had shown up that inside the sanctuary, it was standing room only. People were standing outside unable to get in. It was a great testament to the love felt for this young man, even after his death.

When we saw how many people there were, we decided that after the church service was over, we would let the family go to the graveside by themselves. We would go to a near by restaurant, eat together, then say our goodbyes. However, when the service was over, we faced a great challenge. If my brother and me sat in our cars and let everyone leave and then head to the restaurant, half of the funeral precession would not be able to pass us. The cars packed to tightly into the small streets caused a jumbled mass of Detroit steel and tree shaped air fresheners. Therefore, we decided to travel with the funeral until we could break free, and then head to the restaurant. We got in line and went as far as a red light. When the funeral turned left, we went straight ahead. We got about a mile down the road and I looked into the rear view mirror and saw a horrifying site. Instead of turning at the light, the precession was still following us. Therefore, I called my brother who was ahead of me and told him what was going on. He freaked out, stopped in the middle of the road, ran back to the first car, and told them what had happened. I cannot be sure, but I think that person wanted to kill us.

We got everyone turned around, but not before every person that could, let us know how they felt about us. It was not a shining moment for the Kersey boys. It was a typical moment, but not a shining moment. I can look back and laugh now, but back then, I would cringe when I thought about it. However, I learned two things that day. First, I learned a lot of sign language, and second, we need to keep an eye on our life. Whether we intended it or not someone is following our example. You do not have to be a pastor or a Sunday school teacher to have an influence on someone's life. All you have to do be is around someone, and your life can influence theirs. The greatest influence we have is on those who live in our home. Have you ever noticed that in 1 Timothy chapter three, it talks about the Biblical standards for the bishops and deacons, or in other words, the leadership of the church? What is interesting about this portion of scripture is that it not only outlines the behavior of the leadership, but it also touches on the behavior of our children as well. Take for instance 1 Timothy 3:4-5 "One that rulleth well his own house, having his children in subjection with all gravity. (For if a man know not how to rule his own house, how shall he take care of the church of God?)" (KJV) Why is that? Because our children tend to be a mirror that we can look in, and see how we conduct ourselves when the church is not watching. We tend to be who we really are when our family around.

It is not to say that a child will not rebel against his or her teachings, but children tend to follow our example a little closer than we think. If you want to be a Christian leader, then start at home. If you want to be a Christian at all, begin at home. If you cannot teach your own household how to live right, you will never teach affectively at the church house. If you cannot live right in front of your family, one day you will slip up outside your home, and show the world your true self. We cannot raise a church to love God, if we cannot raise our family to love him. I have to be a Christian leader at home, before I can be one elsewhere. If you are not a leader at home, then you are not a leader anywhere. It is never too late to step up and lead your family in a Godly manner. One of the greatest testimonies that we can pass on to our children is rising above our failures. When our children see us fail, and then do nothing to improve, they too will adopt this lifestyle. They become a generation that never experiences the overcoming power of the Holy Spirit. In order to overcome drug addiction, we must first realize the need to overcome drug addiction. That is what happens when Christ enters our heart. He shows us the need to overcome sin in our life. If we are not very careful, we will teach the younger generation to ignore the Holy Spirit when he convicts us of sin, therefore living a life that is never free from sin.

The prospect of our children never overcoming sin through the Blood of Jesus Christ should terrify even the stoutest heart. That is why it is so important that Jesus be living in, and through us. Jesus is the greatest example that our children have. One of the greatest lessons that the older generation has pointed out to me comes from Christ tempted of Satan. Satan showed Jesus all the kingdoms of the world, and then told him he could have them if he would bow down and worship Satan. Matthew 4:8 says, "Again the devil taketh him into an exceeding high mountain, and sheweth him all the kingdoms of the world, and the glory of them." (KJV) The example that Christ set here is unprecedented. There is glory that comes with all the kingdoms of the world, but it does not compare to the glory that the Father has waiting for those who obey his will. He showed us that even if Satan would give us all the kingdoms of the world, he was still not worth bowing down too. What Satan offers is only temporary, what God offers is eternal. If you are truly concerned about the future of your children, give them an inheritance of eternal things. If we try to raise our children according to the ways of the flesh, we will destroy them. Before I get behind a pulpit, I pray that God will anoint me to speak his word to his people. I have gotten where I ask God for the same anointing when speaking to my children.

Our children deserve the best, and the best is Jesus Christ. And a lot of parents will say that it's not necessary to talk to their children under the anointing of God. However, that is exactly the way they want me to talk when I go visit their children in the jailhouse. We should do the right thing before the wrong thing happens. When a man has major league aspirations for his son, does he teach him how to strike out instead of hitting a homerun? No, he teaches him how to keep his eye on the ball and hit it out of the ballpark. We should take this same approach when teaching our children how to live for God. We are teaching them to strike out in their walk with God, by not teaching them anything. The best teaching method we have is living the life in front of them. Many parents see raising children to love and serve God as an impossible task. That is a lie from the devil himself. When raising a child to serve God, think of it like this. If I wanted to hire someone to teach my child how to play baseball, I would not go and seek out Tiger Woods for the job, even though he is one of the world's top golfers. If I wanted someone to teach them baseball, I would find a baseball player such as Chipper Jones.

Just as it takes a baseball player to teach someone baseball, it takes a Christian to teach someone how to live the Christian life. If you want to teach your children how to live as a Christian, become one yourself. We cannot afford to settle for second best when it comes to teaching our children. If you are trying to live for God and continue in sin, you are giving them your leftovers. We need to be thinking about where our children will be spending eternity. Listen friend, my life has been marked over the years by tragedy, and these tragedies began at an early age. My father was a truck driver who hauled livestock from here in Georgia to Tennessee, Pennsylvania, and other places. He was a very hard working man who stayed on the road a lot, and it caused some strain between him and my mother. Instead of just giving up and throwing away their marriage, they decided to do everything they could to save it. The only problem was dad was always on the road so they did not see each other. Therefore, mom decided that it was time to take drastic measures and take a trip with him on the truck so they could work things out. Keep in mind the trucking industry is a lot different from what it use to be.

Today, most companies will not allow a driver to bring a passenger along unless they are of a certain age and a family member. Some will not allow passengers at all. Nevertheless, back in the 1970s things where not as strict, so Mom not only went on the truck with my father, she brought my brother and me along as well. Some would question this later but mom was doing what she felt were right. I will always defend her actions. While on the road, things went very well. They would talk all the way to Tennessee, and would make strides in reconciling their differences. She would tell me years later that they had decided things would be dramatically different when they got home. It was as if they fell in love all over again on there way to Tennessee. She thanks God everyday since, for the forgiveness, they each found in the love they held for one another. What happened in the coming hours would change our little family forever. Imagine for a moment, a family of four inside the cab of an eighteen-wheeler, hauling a load of cows. It was a cab over truck, which means it did not have the long hood you see on conventional trucks. It would have a flat nose, as some call it, and the driver is actually sitting on top of the engine compartment.

I do not know how hauling livestock is today, but back then, it was a risky business. Cows were not a stable load. If you turned a curb to sharp, or slammed on brakes to fast, the entire load would shift to one part of the trailer, which could be dangerous at best. We were cruising along at a comfortable speed when the unthinkable happened. We topped a hill; and there standing in the middle of the road was a horse. Daddy did not have time to react before he hit the horse driving the bumper into the steer tire, thereby sealing his fate. There was no way for him to control which way the truck went. We slid of the road, hitting a light pole, and then an embankment. When we hit the light pole, it came through the windshield killing my father instantly. Then hitting the embankment caused all the cows to shift to the front of the trailer. The trailer would break free, and actually come over the cab of the truck crushing us underneath. My brother thrown from the truck, and my mother left with just the upper half of her body sticking out. Mom has tried to describe the scene of the crash but I am not sure words can do justice to what she actually saw.

The part of the truck, which held my father, was spilling blood to the ground like an open faucet. Cows were scrambling about, screaming, and bellowing from the injuries they had sustained. Many would have to be put down. When mom tells me of what she saw it scares me half to death, but it shows the mercy of God can shine through any situation. She said she called for my brother, and when she heard him, she looked, and saw him standing close to the truck. Cows were falling out of the trailer landing all around him, because the trailer was still on top of the truck. Therefore, she called him to her, and held him until rescue officials arrived. It took hours to recover the body of my father, but in the mean time, they took my mother and brother to the hospital. Now through all the injuries my mother sustained, she was still continence when help arrived, and I am not sure how things would have turned out for me, if she had not been. There was no one else who could tell them I was still in the truck, my brother only two years old himself. I cannot tell you how long it took them to find me. When the wreck happened, I was asleep in the sleeper, and when the trailer came over the truck, it rolled my up in the mattress, and then crushed me between the top of the cab and the floorboard. When recovered from the truck, I was taken to a hospital in Chattanooga, with a severe head injury.

Now this is what I want you to pay attention too. I was not only taken to the hospital after my mother had left the scene, but I was taken to a different hospital than she. While she lay in the E.R. at another hospital, she knew that her husband was dead; she had seen him. However, she had no idea if I was alive or not. And she tells me that it was devastating to know that she had just lost her husband, but nothing could hold a candle to what was about to happen. As the doctors were working on her trying to stop any bleeding and repair all the broken bones, she over heard someone say that they had recovered the body of a little baby out of the wreckage, and they thought he was dead. Now the doctors had an even greater challenge on there hands. At this point, mom went into shock and nearly died from the news that one of her sons had not made it. She said it was bad enough to loose her man, but to loose a child was a different ball game all together. She was sedated until she found out that I was still alive. Years after I wrecked in 2001, I would see many similarities between the wreck that I was in, and that of my father. We both hit a light pole, we were both twenty-three years old, we both had two children, and they both involve a horse, because mine happened across the road from a horse stable. In addition, in both cases, mom had to be sedated because of me.

Listening to my mother tell the story of all this is heart breaking. It has always terrified me to think of losing one of my children. One night I had a dream that my son had died and I remember waking up in an almost state of shock. My heart was racing, and I could not speak. I tried to stand up and I felt dizzy and fuzzy headed. It would eventually pass; but the feeling of terror would last days after the dream. I thought about that dream long and hard and I came to one conclusion. I do not know how well I could function in life without Gods help if one of my children died; however, something scares me even more than that. What scares me most is one of my children living and breathing beside me, but lost and undone without God. I cannot live with the thought of one of my children not living for God. It is unbearable. Because, God help me if I ever loose one of them, at least I can find comfort in the fact that they are in heaven with the Father, and can someday see them again. That is why we must live this life in front of the next generation. If we do not, we not only loose them here, we loose them in eternity.

CHAPTER TEN

WHAT DON'T KILL YOU, WILL MAKE YOU RUN

Even though I have had a lot of tragedy in my life, I can honestly say that I am a blessed man. I have lived to see God really bless his people, and he is not finished yet. In addition, as along as we stay faithful to him, we can rest assure that his blessing will always be there for our children and us as well. Nevertheless, we must remain faithful, and be vigilant in our walk with God. We must never let down our guard for one minute. What you do has lasting and reaching affects. When I was a young boy about seven or eight years old, I went out into the woods to play as I did most days during the summer. I loved it out in the woods. It was quiet, and peaceful, and most of all it was away from the chores I had to do at home. Sometimes I would dress up like an army man, go out, and fight an imaginary enemy. Other times I would carry my binoculars and watch the birds and squirrels. It was like my second home. However, one day while out there, I would learn first hand how the actions of someone else would cause harm to my life. It was a hot and dry summer day, so I went to the woods to walk around in the shade and enjoy the wind blowing through the pine trees. I had been out there just a short while when I noticed smoke coming from the north of where I was standing.

I thought to myself that someone must have been burning leaves on the other side of the woods, and I was right. The thing is, the man who was burning the leaves let it get away from him. The fire swept through the woods strait towards me. When I saw it coming, I ran to a clear spot where the fire could not reach me. Unfortunately, on the edge of the small clearing I had ran to, was several junk cars that had been left back there years before. This would not have been a problem except the tires on the cars caught fire and started popping. The fire had surrounded me by this time so I had to inch closer to the junk cars, when one of the tires nearest to me popped, shooting flaming hot rubber all over both my arms and my left leg. Let me tell you something here friend. Fire or no fire, it was time to pull up stakes and leave from there. The roadrunner had nothing on me. I ran as hard as I could through those burning woods into women's yard, and that is where I collapsed. Never in your life have you heard screaming as I did that day. I still bear the scars on my body from the actions of a man who did not even know I was in the woods, but he burnt me anyhow.

That man has never laid eyes on me, nor have I ever seen him. Nevertheless, I get to see his handy work every day of my life. And I am not bitter towards that man, it could happen to any of us. It made me realize that my mistakes are not just hurting me. As we walk this Christian way, we need to keep something in mind. When we get offended and start running down the preacher and the church folks with our children sitting in front of us, it will have lasting affects. We seem to forget sometimes that we are going to give an account for every word that falls from our lips. That includes those that cause our children never to return to church. I want you to keep this in mind. We have lead drug addicts, drug dealers, prostitutes, and anyone else imaginable to the Lord, but I have never won a child whose parents went to church, and steady ran the church down in from of them. These children are a closed book. It is as if they are indoctrinated to believe that if you go to church, there is something bad about you, and you cannot be trusted. I am not saying that we cannot reach these people, but I am saying that every time I speak to one it is like talking to a brick wall. If you have a problem with the church, pray about it. Do not run the church down in front of your family, then sit there, and wonder why they will not go to service with you.

The best thing to do is not have a problem with the church in the first place. I cannot understand the human condition when it pertains to going to church. I have seen people who put up with all kinds of stuff on there job and keep going back day after day. They walk through this world all tough and can handle anything, but when they come to church, they act like babies and get offended about every little thing. Its time that the Christians take off their diapers, and slip into some big boy britches, and quit acting like a bunch of spoiled brats who always have to have their way. Not everyone acts this way, matter of fact it is just a few. However, the few do more damage than most pastors can repair. That is why we are seeing a decline in pastors today. No matter how hard we try, we cannot get through to some people. They hang around the church to cause drama, tearing down what the pastor has built up. However, we must not let this kind of behavior discourage us from living for God ourselves, and passing a Godly heritage on to our children. Let us pray for the people who are causing drama in our churches. God has a way of taking care of this type of person, but we must remain faithful and keep our eyes on him.

Let us teach our children to rise above the behavior of those in the church who cause division. In addition, learn how to be peacemakers in this world. Jesus said in the Sermon on the Mount, "Blessed are the peacemakers for they shall be called the children of God" Matthew 5:9. (KJV) We need to start building strong churches. The only way we are going to accomplish this is through unity. The people we are trying to reach with the gospel have seen enough division in the world they are living in; they do not need to see it in the church also. The church should be a place of refuge. It is a place where people should find us truly worshiping God. There is no greater power on this earth than people coming together to worship God, who truly love one another. In addition, the greatest thing that we can pass on to our children is the ability through the cross of Calvary to love unconditionally. Love should come easier to a Christian than any other person on the planet. God is love and we are supposed to be overflowing with him. Love should not be something we have to muster up, but something that flows from us like a well springing up unto everlasting life. And you may wonder how we will ever see love like this while living in the world we live in today, but all things are possible with God.

You can begin bringing love and unity to your church body by starting right where you live. Your home should be top priority in your life. What goes on in your home is a reflection of what goes on between you and God. I have read the book of Nehemiah many times over the years. Something that never ceases to amazes me is the condition of Jerusalem when Nehemiah arrived there. The walls deteariated torn down, so any old thing could just come in and out, as it pleased. Is that the way your home is? Is anything and everything coming in and out of your home as it pleases? Is the television bringing lust and immorality into your home? Is the computer bringing gossip and division into your home, because you had rather talk with someone you knew years ago than talk to your spouse sitting across the room from you? Is your marriage under strain because pornography exists on your computer, but you cannot seem to shake the urge to look at it, despite the fact that it will cost you your marriage? Are you putting the liquor in the top of the cabinet, thinking that your children do not see what you are doing?

I want you to think about this for a moment. The wall of Jerusalem being broken down was the symptom of a greater problem. A lack of brick masons to repair the wall, or carpenters to repair the gates, was not the problem. The problem stemmed from the fact that the people had strayed so far from God that they did not care if the walls were broken down. They had learned to live with, and enjoy what was coming through the walls. I remember walking into the home of a brother in the church one time and they were sitting and watching a movie. Every fourth or fifth word was a cuss word. The saddest part was the little children watching it with them. I can remember when this brother would not allow stuff like this in his home; much less, let his children watch it. And I remember what he said about why he was watching it. He said that there was a time that he would not let stuff like that in his home, but he got were it did not bother him like it use to. Therefore, he started doing it all the time. He got where it did not mater if nudity came on the television, as long as the little kids did not see it. Friend, we need to keep a vigilant watch on what we are allowing into our homes.

Our young men have enough going against them without us allowing a parade of half-naked and all naked women to pass in front of them. In addition, our young women, God help our young women. I don't know about you friend, but I refuse to raise a daughter who feels that the only way she can get the attention of a young man, or get him to love her is to perform some type of sexual act for him. That is what this world is feeding them. My wife saw something one time and it made us just sit down and pray for this generation of young people that is coming up. We pastured a church in a small town, and we were often out in the community getting to know the people there. We got to know this little girl, and she was the sweetest acting child you will ever meet. And understand, this little girl was plump and had a round face. She was short and she did not feel that she was very pretty. And one day my wife is standing inside a convenience store waiting to pay for some items, when this little girl came in the door and started talking to my wife. While they were standing there talking, the little girl stopped talking for a second, pointed over to magazine rack, and said, "Sister Mary, that's who I want to be when I grow up".

My wife turned around there sat a magazine with a woman in a bikini bending over in a pose on the front of it. My wife knelt down beside this child, and in tears explained to her that she was pretty just the way she was. She did not have to dress like that in order to be pretty. This little girl told my wife that she had seen women on television that looked like that, and she wanted to be just like them. Let me tell you something Christian, this world does not have the right to speak into the minds of our children. I know we cannot shield them from the whole world, but we do not have to be shoveling it into our homes either. Let me say it again, we need to defend our homes. We need to pray over our homes, as well as our children. Its time that we as the Church of the Living God stand up for our children and stop letting the world spoon feed filth, and unrighteousness into them. God has entrusted them to us, now its time to protect them with prayer and fasting. Therefore, when Satan does come, he will find a generation prepared to face him wearing the whole armor of God. We cannot take any chances when it comes to the souls of our children. Let us learn to pray, and when we have learned, let us teach our children also.

One thing I noticed in the book of Nehemiah was, the people were coming to him crying because there children were in bondage. They had no way to free them because someone else had possession of their inheritance. Therefore they could not make a living to free their children. That is why protecting our home, and our children, is so important. God gave the inheritance that these people did not have anymore. However, they had let God slip from there lives, and eventually loosing what God had blessed them with. And with the blessing of God gone from there lives, there children soon followed. If we do not keep God fresh and alive in our lives and in our homes, we will soon loose a generation of young people who would have been

Generals in the Army of God. We not only need to wake up, we need to pay attention. We need to have the same burden for our young people that Nehemiah had for the people of Israel. We need to face the facts. We are not always going to be around to tell these young folks how to fight the good fight, so they can carry on after we are gone.

I cannot speak for any other preacher but I do know one thing about myself. I am just a simple gospel gunslinger from the back woods of nowhere. I am not a rich man. The only valuable thing that I can leave my children after I am gone is the Gospel of Jesus Christ. If I am going to leave that legacy behind when I am gone, I have to live it while I am here. I have to live it, before I can leave it. I have the utmost respect for our elderly generation. Their contributions to our country and our churches will never get the full recognition they deserve. We all have reaped the benefits from them. However, I noticed something one day while I was sitting in a barbershop in my hometown. There was a dozen or so elderly men sitting in there talking, and they started running down the younger generation. They started talking about all the mistakes we had made, and how we are sorry and lazy, and did not know how to do anything. Then they went on to say that, we had no respect for the older generation. I did not say anything that day. However, if I knew then, what I know now, I would have said something. I would stand up and tell them that if they want respect then give us something to respect. It is hard to respect people who steady running you down. We know you have done great things throughout your life, but we do not always know what those things are. All we know is what we see out of you now. If you want us to listen to you, give us something worth listening too. If all we hear is criticism, we are going to turn a deaf ear. We know that you went of to war to fight for our country, and we dearly love you for that. Nevertheless, you need to remember that our generation is fighting wars for you now.

When you tell us that we are lazy and sorry when we are out here working ten to twelve hours a day, do you think we are going to listen to anything else you have to say? Sure, there are many lazy people in our generation, but I seem to remember your generation having its fair share also. I am not trying to rebuke the older generation for anything; if you knew me, you would know how much I respect our older generation. I said these words as a warning to us all. The younger generation don't need us steady putting them down, they need us to steady build them up. This generation needs us to tell them how much we love them, and that they are going to make it despite what the world throws at them. They need to hear as often as we can tell them how much we believe in them. We need to tell them that they are going to be great men and women of God. Moreover, we need to start at home telling our own children how blessed they are for having Jesus Christ living inside of them. They need to hear that we are going to help them with any problem that they have without judgment or unholy ridicule.

It is like my uncle use to tell me, there is more than one way to kill a cat than choking him with bread. "No offence to any cat lovers." The point is, there is more than one way to encourage our young people. We need to find the way, and then do it. We need to meet them in the circumstance they are in, and build a relationship from there. Whatever circumstance they may be in, let us carry Jesus when we meet them there. These kids have a tough row to hoe, but so do we. Let us stay on our knees and keep these young people lifted up before God. Let us be sure that what we teach them, we practice ourselves. What good are empty words? Empty words lead to empty lives. Is that what we want for our children? Is that what we want for the youth in our churches, to go out and live empty lives? They do not have to come to church for that. They can crawl into the back seat of any car and find an empty life. They can give money to any drug dealer and receive an empty life in return. They do not need us for that, there are pimps waiting on every street corner just itching at the chance to give your precious daughter an empty life. Is that what we want for this next generation? Then we had better get down to brass tacks in living for God. If we want to play games when it comes to living for God then you should know that Satan has his own game he plays. It is called pregnant at thirteen, drug addict at sixteen, aids at nineteen, and dead at twenty-five. The house always wins that game.

Our children will have what we teach them to pursue. We as the church need to start teaching our young people how to go after God with everything that is in them. We need to start by doing it ourselves. I have seen some very sleazy behavior out of people who are leaders in their church. You need to get your life right with God, or you need to step down, plain and simple. If you are a leader in the church but you cannot set the example for the rest of the church by obeying the scripture then you need to excuse yourself from that position. By the way, Hebrews 10:25 says "Not forsaking the assembling of ourselves as the manner of some is; but exhorting one another: and so much more, as ye see the day approaching." (KJV) If you cannot teach the saints that coming together in worship and Holy Communion with God is not important, then your witness will always be limited by your amount of faithfulness. We as the church need to step up, and it needs to start with the leadership of the church. However, the problem doses not lie solely with leadership, though much of the church would like to shift the blame that way. Matter of fact, most of the leadership in the church today has dedicated their -lives to the Gospel of Jesus Christ, only to be ridiculed by ungodly people for preaching the truth.

Please do not get the idea that because you are not in leadership in your church you do not have to live a holy life. A holy life is required of every Christian, not just Christian leadership. You will stand before the same God as I and give an account for every single action and word that you uttered in your life. You had better get your sins under the blood of Jesus Christ and then get your tongue under subjection to the Spirit of God and stop the gossip and backbiting. Our children are watching us. That may not mean anything to you, but if you love, your children then teach them how to live for God. The greatest gift we can give a child is being a Godly parent. We should not complain about the condition of America if we are not willing to improve the piece we live on.

CHAPTER ELEVEN

TRUTH

Life is full of challenges. However, God has equipped us to meet and overcome every one of them. We are an overcoming people by nature. This world would be in total disaster if God did not cause Christians to be over comers through the blood of Jesus Christ. There would be no hope left in the world if we could not hope for a better life in Jesus. The work done on the Cross of Calvary will forever be the most important event of humankind. We should always keep that event in mind when facing life. I hope the church never looses site of the work that Jesus accomplished at Calvary. If we ever do, we will cease to be the true church. The church was purchased with the precious blood spilled at the cross. We should never let this world encourage us to take the cross down from our churches. God did not call us to be politically correct, if in doing so, it cost us the truth. Truth is all Christians have. Truth is the greatest treasure we have on earth. Truth is not what we make it; truth is what God is. We cannot change that. Why, because you cannot change God, and believe me friend, you do not want a God that man could change. Man has done enough to pervert the Word of God, what you think they would do if they could change God himself.

And if I could speak to every young person of every generation to come, I would say one thing. Hold on to nothing but the truth. Anything less than the truth is a lie, and anything more than the truth is a lie. The truth is your inheritance given to us by God for handing down to generation after generation through the Gospel of Jesus Christ. Do not let anyone steal your inheritance. There is only one truth, and you must seek that truth with all your heart, soul, and mind.

You will never find truth in the ideas and theories of men. Truth comes from the Father himself. Truth diluted, is not truth. Truth without the Cross-is not truth. Truth without the incarnation of Christ is not truth. Truth without the resurrection is not truth. People will call you narrow minded for standing on the truth and nothing else, but so be it. "Straight is the gait, and narrow is the way, which leadeth unto life". Matthew 7:14 (KJV) When you are talking to someone about scripture and both of you have a different opinion of what that scripture that means, one of you, or both of you are wrong. There cannot be two versions of the same truth. Get on your knees before your God and seek the truth with every fiber of your being. If you do not have the truth then you are passing a lie to your children.

Truth does not come by changing God's word. Truth is God's word. It does not need any help from us. Truth will never come to the Christian heart without the Holy Spirits guidance in your life. Truth will only come when we begin to adhere completely to Gods word and his word alone. Truth will not come by embracing other religions into Christianity. Islam has no place in the Christian doctrine. Neither doses any other religion that teaches anything different then Jesus Christ was the son of God crucified for our sins, arose from the grave on the third day, and is now in heaven interceding to the Father on our behalf. If the Cross of Calvary is not preached, we should not be listening. If a man gets behind a pulpit and preaches, but does not mention the cross and the shed blood of Jesus, afraid that he might offend someone, then we need to quit listening to them as preachers of the Gospel. They are excellent motivational speakers. However, what good is motivation without being motivated to embrace the redemptive work accomplished at Calvary? What is the benefit for the soul when we feel good about ourselves without redemption through the blood of Jesus? It is a false hope. It is "Form of Godliness but denying the power thereof" 2 Timothy 3:5 (KJV)

We cannot preach the Gospel and accommodate the world at the same time. Jesus told us that we would "be hated by all nations for my names sake." Matthew 24:9 (KJV) We cannot change Christianity in order to pacify those who appose it. There are denominations today who are allowing immorality behind their pulpits in order to embrace all humanity. We as the church cannot embrace humanity by alluring them with sin, that's Satan's job. We must first embrace holiness and righteousness ourselves, and then carry it out to a lost and dying world. Moreover, there are changes in the church today but the core of the Gospel is still the primary focus. I go into some churches wearing a suit and I am the one who looks out of place, but that is ok, as long as the truth is there. I prefer a suit; some prefer blue jeans and a tea shirt. We should all prefer the truth to the lies the devil is trying to spoon feed the church. We should not let the difference in the way we dress divide us as Christians, but allow the Gospel to bring us together in unity. I remember when I was young, some churches considered you an outcast if you showed up for service in blue jeans. Now days I am being asked by pastors to take off my suit before I come into a church service.

I was shocked one service when met in the parking lot by a pastor who told me I could not wear a suit into his church. I pointed to a sign over the door that said, "Come as you are". I asked him if that was only for those who wore blue jeans and a tea shirt. I was sitting in another church service one night and the preacher stopped his message long enough to point me out and say that we do not have to wear a suit to be a Christian. It brings tears to my eyes when I think of all the time wasted on foolish behavior, when we could be preaching Jesus to those who are lost. Our focus should be preaching the Gospel not airing our differences. I love listening to the preachers that we have on the radio today. I hate to think what this world would be like if we did not have these men and women of God so easily assessable to us. However, I wish they would stick to the Gospel instead of spending so much time putting down other denominations, and other men of God. You have no idea what confusion you are causing in the hearts and minds of your listeners by doing this. I have so many people who have come to me for help in their own life because you would preach such a wonderful message, and then act so ugly towards other people.

People are turning their radios off because they turned it on to hear the Gospel preached, and what they got was men airing their differences. The truth is being lost in the trivial things of the church. It is not hard for other religions to grow, all they have to do pick up the people that the Christian church has run off by not sticking to the Gospel. Preachers need to learn that the pulpit is not about you, it is about the Cross-and what Jesus Christ wants to do for humanity. It is about a life changing experience to those who hear the words that come from our lips. The Bible says "And ye shall know the truth, and the truth shall make you free". John 8:32 (KJV) Preachers, give them the truth straight from Gods word, and then close your mouth. Your opinion and your pulpit is like oil and water, they do not go together. Let us get back to preaching the gospel. Let us try to bring unity to the Body of Christ, not division. Let us come together as the people of God. We come together we tragedy strikes. We stand against abortion, or homosexuality, and other issues so why not unite before these issues arise? The protestant church is divided and should not be. I am not just talking about denominations. I am talking in general. I have been in very few churches were there was not some type of division amongst the congregation. The only problem with trying to bring divided people together is when you do the first question asked is who is going to be in charge? God should be, however, he is usually the last one asked to fill our leadership positions.

The truth of the Gospel is being muffled by the petty differences of people who need to visit an alter. We are better than this. The Bible teaches us in psalms 92:12 "The righteous shall flourish like the palm tree." (KJV) God wants His people to flourish. Are we flourishing or floundering? There is a powerful message in the palm tree, a man could write a whole book just about this tree. One thing I noticed about the palm tree is that it produces from three hundred to six hundred pounds of fruit in a year's time. That is an abundance of fruit considering it grows where most plants cannot grow. One thing we must realize is the fruit that is growing is not just for the benefit of the tree, it is for those who other wise would starve to death if they could not partake of this nourishment. If we can envision this, we get a clear picture of the walk we have in Christ Jesus. This is not about us; it is about what God wants to do through our life. We need to let God produce fruit in our life that will feed those who are starving for the truth. The church should be a produce stand that the world comes to see, and partake of the wonderful works of a loving and merciful God. They can come and enjoy the works of salvation secured by the blood of the precious Lamb of God. Moreover, need I remind you, the fruit that God produces in our life are fruits of righteousness, not the fruit of sin and unrighteousness?

The fruits of righteousness dose amazing things for our life. It can bring unity back to our churches. It helps people believe the words of the Gospel we speak while we are witnessing. In addition, it drives the point home that God always makes a difference in the life of those who surrender to him. It brings not only the favor of God into your life, but also the favor of man. Let me give you an example. I am a man who despises money and what it dose to people, and what it has done to our society, and our country. Rather we want to admit it or not, we need money to keep our churches up and running. Let us "Render unto Caesar the things which are Caesars, and render unto God the things that are Gods". Matthew 22:21 (KJV) When we first came the building we are now in at Brush Arbor Ministries, we had no money at all. I prayed that God would supply every need and he not only came through, but he did it in a surprising way. I have a brother-in-law that would not go to church even if they were giving away free curly fries. He has a good heart, but for reasons of his own, he dose not will not to go to church anymore. However, when I was getting money up to start this ministry, he gave the first hundred dollars. It did not hurt that I am married to his big sister, but he also believed in the ministry we are doing because he has seen us face hard times and stick it out.

In addition, when we needed a church sign made, another friend of mine not only made the signs, but he would not take a dime for the work or material he supplied. Here again, I cannot get him to commit his life fully to God, but he believes in our ministry because he has seen the fruits of righteousness growing in our life. This man has done more for Brush Arbor Ministries than any single person has. I have a solid oak pulpit to rest on while I am preaching because of this man. By the way, I hope this pulpit will remain with my ministry as long as I am alive, and I hope my great grand children preach off it. It is a fine piece of craftsmanship. In addition, if you are reading this book right now, it is because this man gave me the support and encouragement needed to see the project through. If the fruits of righteousness are growing, the entire world will take notice. There is no supplement for the righteousness of God. Even a wicked person can recognize the righteousness of God in your life. While Jesus Christ walked this Earth, his identity went unknown to many of the people because they did not believe in him. However, when he encountered a person possessed of demons, they would often cry out his name because they knew exactly who he was.

If you are a true born again Christian you will stand out in this world. If you are yielding your life completely to Christ, your life will be a light that shines in the dark places. Never be ashamed of that light. I know it is hard to see your friends walk away from you because you have chosen Jesus as your Lord and Savior. However, when those same friends hit rock bottom from the drugs and alcohol and failed relationships, you will be the one they come to for help. Living for God will not be easy, but it will be worth it. When you see your friends fall into hopelessness and you show them hope in Jesus Christ, your walk will be worth it. When you feed some homeless person instead of going to the wild party, your walk will be worth it to that homeless person. When you witness to a man at work and he gives his life to Christ, your walk will be worth it to the child that he would go home and beat if he where not saved. People will see hope in you if you have a genuine walk with God. People will find comfort in your words if you let Christ speak through you. You are an extraordinary person, now let an extraordinary God show you how to become even greater through his son Jesus Christ. You have a wonderful future ahead of you, if you do not let Satan destroy it before you get there.

God has so many wonderful blessings waiting for you. Enjoy your walk with God and do not make it stressful. If your walk with God becomes stressful, ask God why and let him show you how to walk peacefully. We can walk through trials and tribulations and see hard times and not become stressed if we strengthen our faith in God everyday. When I was a teenager a friend of mine started attending the same church I was and he was saved while there. He and I were so excited about living for God. Anytime the church doors opened, we were there. We travelled all over South Georgia going to revivals and camp meetings. Neither of us had much money and blessed our beat up old rides made it out of the county without breaking down. However, we never knew that our lack of money or impending doom of breaking down was supposed to worry us. We just went to church and trusted God to get us there. That is one of the blessed things about newborn Christians; they have not learned yet how to worry so much. The older people would tell us not to be so childish as to drive so far in a truck that may not make it to the destination. The older people taught us how to worry instead of trusting God. We as Christians do things so backwards. We should be learning how to trust God more everyday, not how to worry more everyday.

Over the years, I have learned through reading Proverbs and other books of the Bible that I do not have to live a life of stress in order to be a mature Christian. Matter of fact, I have learned just how immature grown people look by walking around all stressed out. I have had the perfect excuse for stress over the past eleven years, but I refuse to use it anymore. I use to let the pain I was in keep me knotted up emotionally until I realized that stress only adds to the pain. Stress feeds something other than the peace and promises of God into our life. Stress and worry tell us it cannot be done so we never do it. The promises of God tell us that "I can do all things through Christ which strenghteneth me." Philippians 4:13 (KJV) The reason our walk with God becomes so stressful is we try to take things on ourselves. We never learn to do things through Christ. We need to learn the truth contained in God's word and started living in that truth. Let us learn to walk with God the way God intended us to walk with him. We have so many ideas about how to walk with God and they are getting us nowhere. Look to the scripture to teach you how to live for him and quit getting bogged down and needing victory over ever little thing. Somewhere along the way our walk with God should become about helping, others know God, not us always helping ourselves to God. Many people have made God out to be nothing more than a sugar daddy that they go to when they want a hundred dollars or a new Cadillac.

Let us not cheapen the reason for the cross. We experience salvation not only to spend eternity in heaven with God, but through us, the message of the cross is preached to a lost and dying world. God did not give us what we have so we can go hide behind the curtains and not share it with anyone. Quiet the contrary. Jesus wanted you to have the Father to the extent that he bled and died so we may have access to him. The nature of a Christian is one who wants others to receive salvation as well. Where are you Christian? Where are the men and women who see beyond their own banking accounts into the true need of humanity, salvation through the blood of Jesus Christ? Where are you man of God who is raising up missionaries in the church that will someday reach people who will otherwise perish in their sins? Where are you young person who will save the life of your teammate at school by turning them towards God and away from drugs and eventual suicide? This world desperately needs you Christian, so stop sinning and start living up to your full potential in Christ. Search for the truth in God's word with all of your heart soul and mind. And when you find it, share it with someone else.

CHAPTER TWELVE

AN EAGLE RISING

Friend, I believe in you. I believe in the work that God is doing through you. We may face hard times when laboring for the Gospel, but I believe that you have the courage and faith in God to see it through. I know that whatever sin may arise in your life that you will rise above it. I know that whatever weaknesses you have in your life that you are going to trust in God and hold on to that faith until you have the victory you need. You are an eagle rising. You are an eagle rising above the compromise the people around you are falling into everyday. You are an eagle rising above the troubles and cares of a world that will chew you up and spit you out. You are an eagle rising to the occasion, when the occasion calls for a man or women of God who refuses to compromise when faced with loneness, persecution, or even death. When things arise in your life that calls for you to compromise your belief in your God and your Savior, I want you to realize that these are some of the most important times in your Christian walk. You may feel at that moment that you cannot stand and will surly fall, but remember, "They that wait upon the Lord shall renew their strength, they shall mount up with wings as eagles." Isaiah 40:31 (KJV) When you need strength do not depend upon your own but turn to God to receive a strength that endures for eternity. The strength that God gives never fades away only gets stronger as you yield yourself even more to him. "Not by might, nor by power, but by my spirit, saith the Lord of host." Zechariah 4:6 (KJV) The less of you there is the more of God there will be in your life. The more of God you have, the more victory you have.

I am no expert on eagles, I have read about them over the years, but I am not an expert. Nevertheless, I do know one thing about them. I have seen eagles in the wild, and they fly like no other bird. Here in South Georgia we have an abundance of hawks. We may see three or four on our way to the church on Sunday. They are beautiful birds. You can tell when they are flying whether it is a hawk flying or not. They have a very distinctive way of flying. However, the flight of the Eagle is even more majestic than the Red-tailed Hawk. The flight of the Eagle makes a statement about the mindset and determination of that bird. It says that he knows he is different, therefore; he does not try to act like other birds. He finds his distinction in the way God made him, not conforming to something outside of Gods plan. That is who you are. You find your distinction in God's design. I had a truck years ago that I loved a lot. It was a good-looking truck. People would ask me how I got that truck to look so good and the explanation was simple. All the other guys around town would change the grill of their truck, or the bumpers, or they would raise it or lower it. However, my truck was original equipment. I did not change anything except the wheels; I went with a ten-inch wide rim to set the truck off. Nevertheless, as far as the truck itself was concerned, I did not change a thing.

I know we as human beings are looking for a way to be different so we do not fade into a background of Polo shirts, and holy jeans. However, if you want to be different in this world, try the original equipment. If you become what God designed you to be, I assure you, you will soar differently than any bird that is in the sky. I have faith that you will become the original equipment. I expect no less of you. You will rise above the opinion that your family has of you. You will rise above the feelings of inadequacy that people fed into you. You are what you allow God to form in you, not what man has bent and twisted you into. We need to walk in the assurance that we do not have to live up the low expectations of the world, but we are the people of God, therefore, in the world, not part of the world. Keep in mind the story of David pursued by King Saul in First Samuel chapter twenty-four. Saul had tried to kill David unsuccessfully several times. In his pursuit, Saul finds a small cave in which he enters to cover his feet. What Saul does not realize is that David and several of his men are hiding inside this very same cave. As Saul is doing his thing, David's men suggest to David that he kill Saul while he has the chance. However, instead of killing Saul David chooses the high road and cuts the edge off Saul's garment that he is wearing.

It seemed right the eyes of everyone around David for him to kill Saul and rid himself of having to run for his life every waking moment. David did not see it that way and that is why the Bible refers to David as a man after God's own heart. David would rather show mercy than avenge himself of those who had wronged him. We need to cease doing what feels right or what seems right and start doing what God tells us to do in his Holy word. What seems right in the eyes of man rarely lines up with God's word, so let us obey God's word and nothing else. David did not listen to the voices around him; he chose to please God rather than please the men at his side. Moreover, to bring it closer to home, we may have to please God instead of pleasing our spouse. We may have to please God over pleasing our friends. Why should we please God instead of pleasing our spouse or our friends? Because like David's men, they need someone who is making Godly decisions not decisions based upon emotions not grounded in the Spirit of God. If you only make Godly decisions then you will only make the right decisions. Decisions rooted in God's word can only bring forth positive results, and fruits of righteousness. It is time you start making Godly decisions and stop letting the flesh get in the way of what God is trying to do at your church, your home, and in your life.

The story of Saul and David illustrates another point as well. When David was a boy and went on a battlefield to face a giant, King Saul was part of that generation who was hiding in the tents. The man who was in a position to be a great influence in David's life became a distraction more than an encouragement. The saddest part of the story is this kind of behavior is still alive and well in our churches today. I will give you two examples. The first example is evident if you look at who is standing behind the pulpits in the American church today. Many denominations are recognizing that fewer young people are standing behind this sacred desk, and some denominations are asking their retired preachers to begin pasturing again because they have no one else to do it. Why is this happening? I can give you several reasons; however, I would like to highlight just one. One reason we are seeing such a decline in young ministers is that if they are any good, they are seen as a threat to some of the older preachers around them. Washington D.C. cannot hold a candle to the politics that go on in the ministry today. I have seen preachers do some dirty things to one another just so they can get a higher position in their denomination, or get a bigger church. In addition, some do hateful things out of pride for their position in the ministry. I had the pastor of a prominent church in a near by town ask me to go on the radio with him after I had spoken at his church.

He said that his congregation had enjoyed the message and he was well pleased with the results of the service and thought this same enthusiasm would carry over well to his radio program. I unfortunately had to decline his invitation because of a prior engagement. This pastor was so mad at me for not doing what he asked that he showed a side of himself that was nowhere near Christ like. His language was unbecoming a Christian much less a man of God. Andrew Dice Clay had nothing on this man. He told me how long he had been a pastor and named all the positions he had held with his denomination, and how dare I not accept his invitation. He did not stop there. He got up the next Sunday and publicly denounced my ministry and me. All because he thought that, someone so young should not decline the invitation of someone who had been in the ministry as long as he had. Several years later, he became a state overseer for his denomination. Is it any wonder I am writing a book about rising above? You may have to face a Saul in your walk with God. The question is how you will react when it happens. David reacted well by not killing Saul. I cannot say that he acted perfectly because he did cut part of his garment off. However, in doing this David could hold up evidence of a life that Saul should be living because it was still a fragment of a king's garment.

David was reminding Saul that he still occupied a place of leadership handed to him by God and as long as he held that position, he needed to act in a manner suited to that Godly position. It is sad that all David got from Saul was a torn rag and bad memories. Saul could have helped David so much, but David took his lessons from God. You have to stand when no one else will and take your lessons from God. This brings me to number two on our list of ways that Saul's behavior still exists in the church today. Saul grew jealous of the victories that David had won and the attention that it brought him. The people would sing about Saul killing his thousands and David his ten thousand. David knew, as you need to know, that the more battles that are won the safer our families will be. You need to win all the spiritual battles that lie in front of you and do not let anyone discourage you from doing so. You may overcome something that someone else has been struggling with for years and it may bother them, however do not let that stop you from overcoming the next item on the list. You yield yourself completely to the power of the Holy Spirit and let God handle those that may become jealous of your walk with God. Find some well-rounded friends that you can depend upon and uplift one another as often as you can. There are too many good people in the church for you to allow the Saul to ruin your walk with God. It took me a while to figure that out, but once I did, my life took on a very different light.

Do not let Saul discourage you. Your Saul maybe the church you are pasturing. The battle you are wining maybe seeing your church grow, and few if any in that church may share your vision. I have seen pastors young and old who wanted to bring revival to a church and see the church grow by people coming and being saved. And these same pastors are given the option of quieting down and leaving things the way they are, or losing their job. Do not ever quiet down preaching the gospel and seeing souls saved. Moreover, do not ever leave things the way they are if it is not the plan of God for things to be that way. Fall on your knees and begin to pray for your church. God has a way of changing people's minds. If they do not want to change, do not give up. God will open a door for you. I know of churches who are hungry for revival and they are tired of seeing empty pews. Stand strong when it comes to your faith in God and doing what he has called you to do. It will all be worth it. Serving God is a wonderful thing. It is the best thing you will ever do in your life. I know you are going to overcome everything that comes your way and you will do it through the blood of Jesus Christ. Saul has no say so in your life and neither dose Satan. This is between you and your Father in Heaven so focus on him and nothing else. All Saul wants to do is divert your focus to something other than God. Do not let this happen. You are better than that. You are an Eagle rising.

If God is to be the focus, you must keep your prayer time top priority in your life followed by the study of scripture. You may say, "David, my family comes first and is top priority in my life". However, you are of little or no value to your family if you do not put God first above everything else. They need to see you living the life of a Christian everyday. I hear people say that the good people always finish last. If that is true, it is because we stopped to help those who fell along the way. And why do we do this kind of thing with no regard to whether we finish first or last in this world? It is Christian nature to reach out to any and everyone that needs a helping hand. We have a generation in front of us who is waiting for us to pick them up and show them how to live for God. We are raising a generation who needs to see us stand for Christ more now than we ever have. The greatest way we can make a stand for Jesus Christ here in this world of sin and corruption is by falling on our knees. On our knees is where we will find those who have fallen into sin. On our knees is where we can embrace our little children and see them eye to eye. This is where we can wash the feet of those who may betray us; however, we will love them and show kindness towards them nonetheless. Jesus knew what Judas would do but he washed his feet along with the others. If you want to see the knees of Satan and every demon of hell sake with fear, just fall on yours and begin to cry out to your Father in heaven. The legs are what keep us mobile and able to go where we want to go and move at what pace we want to move. When on our knees, the legs are bent to the point of immobility. Only then, can we understand the strength and guidance the Father gives us. He does not need our strength to move us; we need his strength in order to move in His Spirit. On our knees, we learn the true meaning of being a man or a woman.

On our knees, we can see over the valley into the mountaintop above. On our knees, we can see that person who has fallen and needs us to help them get up again. I hope our children see this kind of life style out of us. One that says if you fall, I will be there to pick you up. We need to be sure to teach our children this way of life. If they do not learn to minister to those who fall, then the world will eventually raise a fallen generation who never gets up. That cannot happen. That is why God has sent us into the hedges and highways, because that is where the world is throwing its castaways. Moreover, the world's castaways are a pearl of great price to Jesus Christ. Before you go out into this world to spread the Gospel of Jesus Christ, let me encourage you to read the first chapter of the book of Joshua. Notice Joshua 1:5 "There shall not any man be able to stand before thee all the days of thy life: as I was with Moses, so I will be with thee: I will not fail thee, nor forsake thee." (KJV) As you read on to Joshua 1:6 it says "Be strong and of a good courage." (KJV) In addition, Joshua 1:7 repeats the message "Only be thou strong and very courageous." (KJV) That is the message I would like to leave with you my dear friend. No matter what comes your way, no matter how bad you want to give up, just remember these words. Be strong and of good courage.